Life as Eucharist

Also by Norman Pittenger:

Life in Christ

Life as Eucharist

by

NORMAN PITTENGER

WILLIAM B. EERDMANS PUBLISHING COMPANY
Grand Rapids, Michigan

Library of Congress Cataloging in Publication Data

Pittenger, William Norman, 1905-
Life as Eucharist.

Based on lectures given in Amarillo, Tex.,
Mar., 1972.
1. Lord's Supper. I. Title.
BV825.2.P57   234'.163   73-7765 JUL   3 '74
ISBN 0-8028-1542-1

Prefatory Note

In March, 1972, during a lecture trip to the United States, I had the unusual pleasure of giving a set of lectures at a conference of Roman Catholic clergy in Amarillo, Texas. The invitation to deliver these lectures was a surprise, but a most gratifying one. Furthermore, the fact that the committee in charge asked me "to talk to them about the Mass" — the usual Roman Catholic name for the Lord's Supper, Holy Communion, or Eucharist — was particularly gratifying.

This small book contains the lectures which I gave in Amarillo, with some slight expansion here and there. My purpose was to discuss the central action of Christian worship in an ecumenical spirit, trying to find and consider the points on which almost all who "profess and call themselves Christian" can and do agree. I cannot say whether I have succeeded in this purpose, but I *can* say that the Roman Catholic clergy seemed to find little with which they disagreed, while later on when I presented the same material to a group of non-Roman Catholics (including Congregationalists, Presbyterians, Methodists, Disciples, as well as Episcopalians) the members of that group were good enough to tell me that they were almost completely in accord.

All this seems encouraging to me. If there is one thing

that is taken to separate Christians of various persuasions, it is their interpretation of Holy Communion. But I am now convinced that much, if not all, of the problem is to be found in the words used to describe the significance of that chief act of worship. If these lectures, now a small book, help anybody to penetrate beneath words to abiding meaning, I shall be rewarded abundantly for what I have tried to do.

Finally, I must thank the clergy who asked me to speak and listened to me during those delightful three days in northwest Texas. Their friendliness, openness, ready hospitality, and generosity of spirit will always remain in my memory.

King's College   Norman Pittenger
Cambridge, England

P.S. The "theological appendix," originally an article in *Christian Renewal* and not included in the lectures in Texas, is reprinted by the kind permission of the editor.

Contents

Prefatory Note 5

1. The Church as the Body of Christ 9

2. The Eucharist: Divine Action in Human Action 22

3. The Priesthood of the People of God 35

4. The Eucharist and the Christian Man 47

5. The Eucharist and Social Awareness 59

6. The Eucharist and Christian Action 71

7. Life in Christ in the Body of Christ 88

A Theological Appendix 93

1
The Church as the Body of Christ

As we all know, the word "community" is in the air these days. We hear of the need for "community" in fulfilling our human lives and realizing our human potentialities. There is a demand for "world community" as the one way towards international understanding. "Community service" is the term often employed for what was once called "social service." And even in philosophical discussion, "community" has come to be a key word, used to describe the solidarity and mutuality that are found at every level of life and experience. All these are instances of a new feeling that has seized the imaginations of large numbers of people in all parts of the world. "Togetherness," we have been brought to believe, is of the very essence of existence. And that awareness is sweeping over the whole world, as we turn or seek to turn from *laissez-faire* individualism and self-defeating isolationism towards a corporate and cooperative planetary life.

Parallel with this concern in secular fields for "community," there is a significant trend in Christian thinking that is equally devoted to the feeling for "community." This is the deepening of Christian understanding of the meaning of life "in Christ" in the fellowship of the faith-ful. No more important fact can be discerned in the Christian Church's theology during recent years. There was a time when many who called themselves Christian seemed content to accept the idea that the Church is a gathering of individuals, each of them individually re-lated to God and united in a single organization merely by reason of certain beliefs they all hold, certain prac-tices they all adopt, and certain behavior patterns they all try to follow. Even in circles that were self-consciously "Catholic," where the social expression of Christian faith would inevitably be central, there was often the idea that the Church possessed only a mechanical, formal, and static unity. Far from being regarded as an organic, vital, dynamic movement, the Church was seen as more like a machine that had been set in operation by God in Jesus Christ, running in a fashion that presumably was pleas-ing to him, even if somehow not quite as effective as one might wish in a world that had greatly changed since the days when the machine was first put into it and (to con-tinue the metaphor) the button pressed to start it going.

But today we find everywhere a very different notion of the Christian Church. Both in traditionally "Catholic" and traditionally "Protestant" circles, the dominant view of the Church's nature is that of a living fellowship of loving souls, a genuine "community" that finds its union in its Lord as Head, its enriching source of life in mem-bership in a body that is *his* Body, its enabling strength from him through the *Una Sancta* (as continental Chris-tians style it) — a striking parallel to the emphasis on "belonging" discovered in secular circles. The emergence of this vitalistic conception of the Church as a living fellowship that is the Body of Christ may well be taken as one of the signal evidences of the working of the Holy Spirit in the history of Christian thought. To all intents and purposes this conception, so deeply grounded in, say, the Johannine and Pauline writing of the New Testament, had been either dead or forgotten for hundreds of years. Then it came to life again, or was remembered; and its impact has changed everything we say or think about the Church, its worship, its faith, and its reason for being. On every hand, from the Bishop of Rome who issued the encyclical on *The Mystical Body of Christ* to the many pronouncements by theologians and the messages sent forth from the World Council of Churches, we find evidence of the renewal of this portrayal of the Christian Church as an organic, bodily, vital, dynamic unity.

The Eastern Orthodox have had their own contribution to make to this growing consensus, not only because their own life so well represents "community-in-love" (which the Russians among them call *sobornoy*) as the heart of Christian life, but also because they have shown that the very word "Catholic," applied to the Church, means in the first instance "organic" or "whole" or "integral," being derived from a Greek phrase that (they tell us) should properly be translated as "according to, or in terms of, the wholeness" — *kath'olou*. The sense of "Catholic" as "universal," they say, is a derivative of this primary meaning; it has significance only when set against this deeper significance of "Catholic."

It hardly requires much demonstration, for anyone familiar with Holy Scripture, that this organic conception of the Church as a living fellowship that is Christ's "Body," as over against an individualistic or mechanistic

[11]

notion, corresponds to our Lord's own thought and to that of the primitive community of believers in him. If we take St. John's Gospel as in any way true to the essential *idea* of Jesus, even if we agree with recent biblical studies that indicate that it does not represent his actual *words,* we cannot avoid the central place that intimate interrelatedness, organic wholeness, held in his mind as to the way in which he and his followers were to be united. The idea is presented with remarkable richness in John 15:1-12. Here the vine and its branches are chosen as the most satisfactory symbol of the relation between Christ and those who respond to him. The vine supplies life to its branches; the latter would wither and die if they lacked that life. They can bring forth fruit only if they are in healthy relationship with the main stem of the vine. The energy that flows through them and causes them to burgeon forth is not their own; it comes from the main stem and belongs to the branches only by gift. "I am the vine, ye are the branches . . . without me, ye can do nothing." So St. John's Gospel presents the thought of our Lord.

In St. Paul's thought, too, the same idea is presented but with the use of another image. Here the motif is that of a body and its members. In I Corinthians 12:1-29 we find perhaps the clearest statement of the point; but everywhere in his epistles it is, so to say, the underlying assumption. The Church is *Christ in and with his members.* It is a body, the Body of Christ himself, to which the members belong. Each Christian exists as such because of his membership in the Body; each brings his particular talents and abilities to be used by the Body; each has his own part and his own place in the Body.

[12]

Christ is the Head of the Body, who ultimately controls it, who seeks expression through it, who makes himself known by means of it. The Body is *one* Body since it has the one Head; its members are united in him because they are united in it, and *vice versa*. Each member is therefore an instrumental agency for the life and the work of the Body as a whole and for the Head who informs that Body. Thus, and in consequence, Christians are members one of another, because they are members of Christ's Body, given the responsibility to bring the life of Christ to the world.

The Christian Church as it is pictured for us in the New Testament is a reality best symbolized and understood in organic images — whether the "model" is of the Temple and its component stones, or a family under one Father, or the Bride of Christ united with the Bridegroom, the same point is being made. But the image of the body with its members, or that of the vine and its branches, seems the most suggestive, perhaps even central. One life flows through the whole reality of the Church: it is the life of Jesus Christ. And that means that it is the life of God himself, the eternal Love that makes and sustains all things, now united inextricably and ineffably with human nature and flowing into the race of men to lift them to the level of "life in love" that *is* "life in God." This level has been called "God-manhood" by the Eastern theologians, for it is given in him who is known as "God-Man," Jesus Christ. St. Paul called it "life in Christ"; we may speak of it as "en-Christed life."

It is amazing to notice how many times in St. Paul's letters the phrase "in Christ" occurs. We have taken it

[13]

so much for granted that we have failed to see its primary place in his thought. For him, it is apparent, to be "in Christ" was the whole meaning of his Christian experience from the moment of his conversion on the Damascus Road. It was the point of that conversion, since there he became "a new man in Christ." It is the key to his theology, for the thought of St. Paul is no systematic scheme of intellectual beliefs but a vivid experience of life "in Christ" that radically altered his way of seeing everything. And since it was St. Paul who also spoke so compellingly of the Christian fellowship as the Body of Christ, we are obliged to relate that portrayal of the Church, which is central to his thought, with the deep sense of life "in Christ" that was central to the man himself.

What St. Paul is really saying is that to be "in Christ" *is* to be "a member of Christ's Body." To be "a member of the Body of Christ" *is* to participate in the life that is "in Christ." The two are not simply interchangeable ideas; they are one and the same thing, seen from different angles. That is why, for example, he can remark in that much misunderstood verse of I Corinthians (11:29) that if we take part in the sacramental meal of the Christian fellowship without "discerning the Lord's Body," we "eat and drink damnation" to ourselves. What St. Paul means here is that those who partake of the Eucharist without recognizing the Lord's Body, which is the *Church* — that is, without the deepest participation in the community where membership in the organic reality of the Christian fellowship is central — are not sharing in the sociality of Christian faith. They are not participant in the intimate interrelatedness with other members of the Body of Christ that is their very exist-

[14]

ence as Christians; hence they are destroying their own participation, they are making the sacrament of "none effect," they do not "discern" the meaning of what they are doing in eucharistic worship. The intimate inter-relatedness *is* being "in Christ," who is himself the life of the fellowship that shares in the sacramental act — it is Christ who shares himself with his members in that Eucharist.

The theme of this book is given in the final words of the last paragraph. Succeeding chapters will seek to work out various aspects and implications of that theme. But for the present we must continue with our discussion of the significance of this basic conception of the Christian fellowship as the Body of Christ and of ourselves as members of that Body. For there are several points that need to be spelled out in more detail, lest the whole position be misunderstood or wrongly applied.

The Christian Church is the level of the "en-Christed" life made available to men; it is nothing other than "life in Love," with the word "Love" given a capital "L" because we are here speaking of God himself who, in Wesley's words, is "pure unbounded love." Now the point of insertion of that life into the world is in Jesus Christ, the Man of Nazareth about whom we read in the New Testament and whose significance is affirmed in Christian faith when he is called the "incarnate Word of God." But we must be clear that in speaking of Jesus Christ as "the point of insertion" we are not suggesting that apart from him there is *no* knowledge of God, *no* sharing in God's life, *no* manifestation of God as Love. Although some Christian theologians have spoken in this arrogant fashion, it is not typically traditional Christian theology to do so. What is in view here is a definitive, decisive, and special, but not an exclusive and confining, moment in the history of God's relationship with men. In the New Testament we are told that God has "nowhere left himself without witness"; we cannot be less generous in spirit than the New Testament itself.

But there *is* something distinctive about "life in Christ"; that distinction is indicated by the very words *in Christ*. St. Paul in using this phrase is talking about a quality of life he knows as identical with that which was the quality of life in Jesus himself. This is self-giving, participant, deeply concerned, and caring love. Thus the level of "en-Christed" life is not self-contained nor introverted; it is a living, growing, expanding, out-ward-moving reality, spreading across the world and down the centuries; and it is known, at least in principle, in the Christian community, which is a fellowship of lovers, lovers of their fellow men and lovers of God in Christ. The fellowship is also living, growing, expanding, for it is indwelt by Christ himself. It has even been suggested by some that this fellowship may be described as Christ in his *social* humanity, just as the Man Jesus, living at a particular time and place, possessed a physical body that was Christ in his *personal* humanity. Perhaps this is not too successful a way of stating it; but the main point is clear: we have to do with the one Christ, for he *is* one, he is not divided.

Now a very serious question may be raised at this point. What about the obvious sin, weakness, and error of the institutional Christian Church? How can one possibly think that the institutional Church is anything like what we have just been describing? In answering that question, we need to be entirely honest. The sin, weakness, and error of the institutional Church must be admitted; these have been, and they still are, plain facts. Only the blind will not recognize them; only those who have been bewitched by mere institutionalism will fail to admit their presence. Christian people, especially those who are most intimately connected with the affairs of the institutional Church, should be prepared shamefacedly to acknowledge and sadly to confess them. We know, or we ought to know, how often the Church in this sense has made mistakes in judgment, failed to be true to its Lord and his gospel, weakly accepted "the world" — in the *bad* sense of that word—and the ways of "the world," rather than valiantly contended for Christian truth, Christian generosity, Christian love, against all comers.

On the other hand, the secret life of the Christian fellowship runs deeper than all these. The Church has its human side, since it is made up, humanly speaking, of men and women at all stages of life and with a great variety of interests, as well as with the defects, the blindnesses, and the cupidity to which human life is prone. They are men and women, then, who remain what they are even when they have become the branches, the members of the true Vine and the true Body. Incorporation into the Christian Church, making them thus true branches and true members, does not work some magical change in them. The dreadful fact must be acknowledged — men are not totally redeemed in their earthly pilgrimage, even if they are set on the way to such perfection as God has intended for them. They are sinful, they are weak, they make mistakes. They do the wrong thing, make the wrong choices, prefer the easier way.

[17]

Since this is the case, it is inevitable that the community itself will also be marked by such defects, limitations, and "diminishments" (as Teilhard would have put it). After all, the fellowship of Christian believers is also a sociological fact; that is the inevitable consequence of its existing in the real world. But like its Lord, the Church may be seen as twofold in nature. Most certainly it has its human side and that side can often be unpleasant. Here it differs from its Lord, who wore his humanity as a royal garment, in all purity and goodness. But it is like him, once again, in having what we may dare to style its divine side. There is the divine reality of the Body of Christ, working through and in the human reality of a sociological organization. The divine reality is there just as truly as the human reality composed of members who both individually and in their groupings are weak, sinful, and erring men.

We believe that as the Body of Christ, in its intended wholeness and purity, as the true Vine and the true Body, the Church is wonderfully indefectible. By that we mean that it is filled with the strength of Christ and in touch with the truth of God. This indefectibility is not apparent all the time; certainly it is not obviously placarded before our eyes. But it is manifested, nonetheless, in the capacity of the Church to reform itself. We can see how the fresh and invigorating life of Christ in his Body has brought the visibly manifest community to recover itself from the errors of various thinkers who could have damaged it terribly. We can notice how the Church was revived through the person and work of St. Francis and his followers in the middle ages. We can see how the Reformation in the sixteenth century removed error. We can observe how Charles and John Wesley did much the same work of revival in the fairly recent past. Today we can see the rediscovery of the sense of Christian unity, the deepening understanding of the imperatives of the gospel, the renewed sense of Christian mission to the world.

Even on its human side, the Christian fellowship has not been, and is not today, permanently or always or everywhere in sin, in error, in disloyalty to its Lord. In the long run, given time and opportunity, it has an astonishing capacity to recover its health. Indeed the Church in this sense is not merely *like* an organism that can get back its health after serious illness; we are permitted to think of it precisely *as* such an organism, whose inner healthy life is the life of Jesus Christ himself, present in it and working through it. It can suffer hurts, fall ill, be grievously stricken; but it does not become victim of a *mortal* disease. This is a matter of Christian faith, of course; but that faith affirms that "in the end," every "spot and blemish" (as the New Testament phrases it) will be done away and there will be a "glorious Church," the perfected 'Body of Christ, to be transfigured into that which all along it has been intended to become — the Bride of Christ.

The responsibility and duty, as also the privilege, of every member of the Church is to be an instrument for exactly that "perfecting" of the Church, under God. This is why many of us continue to "put up with the institution," refuse to "contract out," insist on doing everything in our power to "let the Church *be* the Church." That last phrase was once used by William Temple; it is both apt and compelling.

[19]

Some may think that all this is far too theological for simple believers. To that objection the answer is very simple. Our religion has been terribly damaged during the past century by the absence of a sound and informed theology of the Church. Now we are beginning to recover one. In any event, theology need not be tedious and dull; when it is, it is poor theology. Sound theology demands the use of our minds — and we are coming to learn that we *are* to love God "with our minds" as well as with our hearts and souls and wills. It is essential to true discipleship and informed devotion that we *think;* for theology, in this sense, is like the bone structure of our human bodies — it ensures that we belong to the order of vertebrates. A nontheological religion resembles nothing so much as a jellyfish.

On the other hand, some may think that what we have been saying is altogether too "mystical," by which they will mean "unreal and imaginary." To that objection, too, there is a very simple answer. What we have been saying about the Church as the Body of Christ is indeed "mystical," but in the strictly proper sense of that word. That is, it concerns the inner spiritual reality, the genuine heart stuff, of the Christian fellowship, rather than the outward and obvious appearances. But it is *not* for that reason "unreal and imaginary." It is plain matter-of-fact Christianity.

The old Anglican Prayer of Thanksgiving spoke of the Church as "Christ's *mystical* Body." By this it meant that the Church was hiddenly identified with its Lord. And when any of us comes to think seriously about his Christian faith, he will see that central to it is the community into which he was admitted by baptism. At the heart of his Christian life is the sense of fellowship with Christ and in him with our brethren. The trouble with us, so much of the time, is that we accept this verbally but do not let our imaginations dwell on it, our lives circle around it, our hearts rejoice in it, our wills express it. We are possessors of — or better, we are possessed by— the "en-Christed life" in that fellowship which is Christ's Body and of which he is Head. Let us make this thought central to our daily life and work. Then we may be built up in the Body of Christ, "till we come in the unity of the faith, and of the knowledge of the Son of God, unto a perfect man, unto the measure of the stature of the fulness of Christ."

2

The Eucharist: Divine Action in Human Action

In the Prayer of Oblation, which the Prayer Book of the Episcopal Church in the United States placed in the consecration prayer of the Holy Communion, there are these words: "We thy humble servants do celebrate and make here before thy divine majesty, with these thy holy gifts which we now offer unto thee, the memorial thy Son hath commanded us to make, having in remembrance his blessed passion and precious death, his mighty resurrection and glorious ascension, rendering unto thee most hearty thanks for the innumerable benefits procured unto us by the same."

With variations of phrasing, practically every ancient liturgy of the Church includes some such oblation prayer. And the words make immediately plain to us why it is right to say that the characteristic action of the Church, which as we have seen can only properly be understood as the Body of Christ of which we are members, is found in its *worship*. And not in worship in any way that might occur to us as being interesting or desirable or helpful, but worship in *this* way — eucharistic worship, worship in which we "celebrate and make" before God the Father of all men, by the power of the Holy Spirit who indwells the Church and enables it in all its action, that "memorial" which represents to us the redemptive act of Jesus Christ on our behalf.

As the following chapters will make clear, worship is not to be separated from work. The worship of God is no invitation to escape from the world and from the responsibilities God has given to his human children. Yet worship is primary — and this for reasons that will soon appear. For it is the Christian faith that the divine reality whom we call God, who is the Father of our spirits, the Love that undergirds and acts through the entire cosmos, has given to men a specific relationship with himself through Jesus Christ. He has made available to us the "en-Christed life"; and he has done this by a redemptive act whereby in the person of his Eternal Son made flesh and "in the substance of our mortal nature" — to employ the ancient theological terms — he conquered sin, evil, and death upon the cross. Thereby he established that new level of "life in Christ" into which the human brethren of Jesus are to enter. He "opened to us the gate of heaven" and he prepared for us an eternal destiny. But he did even more. He made available to us, here and now, in this present world where we now live, an entrance into this intended destiny. As in faith and penitence we receive the holy gifts of bread and wine that we have offered to God in union with and as a token of our "remembrance" of the passion and death of Christ on Calvary, we share also in Christ's risen life — we are raised with Christ to "heavenly places" and enabled to live in him as he lives in us.

[23]

Thus if there is anything that is specifically and essentially Christian, it is the celebration of the Eucharist, day by day and week by week, in the context of the life of the Christian Church that is Christ's Body. The Christian *thing,* in G. K. Chesterton's word, is characteristically stated and declared in the "continual remembrance of the sacrifice of the death of Christ," in the sharing in his risen life through communion, and in the fellowship with God in him, and with our brethren through him, in this sacrament of his body and blood.

One of the ancient liturgies includes this prayer, said at the conclusion of the Eucharist: "The mystery of thy dispensation, O Christ, is accomplished so far as in us lies; we have made the memorial of thy death, we have seen the type of thy resurrection, we have been made partakers of thy heavenly table. Of this do thou make us ever more worthy, O Christ, through thy holy and life-giving Spirit." Certainly no prayer is more to the point — we should do well to use it after we have received the sacrament.

The Jesuit George Tyrrell, whose writings were influential in the early years of this century and who (despite the treatment then accorded him by the Roman Catholic Church) is once again being read, once remarked that the Christianity of the future would consist of "mysticism and charity" — of a relationship of men with God and a loving life with their brethren. With this, he associated the Eucharist; and rightly so, for that action *is* relationship with God and love for the brethren. It sums up, as St. Thomas Aquinas once noted, "the whole mystery of our redemption" — and *charity,* or life in a love that generously and freely gives itself, is the total sense of the Christian's existence, the existence of a man who is "in Christ." Eucharist leading to charity in a relationship with God: there is the logic of Christian worship, based (as it must needs be) upon the affirmations of Christian faith. The phrase "based on the Christian faith" is essential here, since where there is no deep and abiding faith in Jesus Christ as God's distinctive action in human life, there can be no Eucharist as true "memorial" and no charity such as was poured out into the world once for all on Calvary's hill.

But what do we do when we celebrate the Eucharist? An answer to that question will show how the Eucharist is exactly what the title of this chapter calls it: the divine action in a human action.

First of all, we *offer*. But what do we offer? The Eucharist is itself an offering, a remembrance or a memorial in which we re-present, in a ceremonial action we are told Christ himself "commanded and taught," all that his life and death and rising again have done for the world. This is indeed a "sacrifice of praise and thanksgiving," as the Prayer Book says. The catechism was right in putting this down *before* it mentioned the fact of its significance as being for "the strengthening and refreshing of our souls." So far as the order of things is concerned, Christian worship in this respect is no different from any other activity of man. Before we can *get,* we must *give;* even if, as is often the case, it is only the willingness and the desire to give and hence to receive God's gift, that we are able really to offer of and by ourselves. We need not give much, for as finite human beings, with all our imperfection, there is little that we have to give. And so far as God is concerned, we can

[25]

indeed give *very* little, beyond our faults and sins repented of and our desire to be more pleasing to him. But God himself gives us something more worthy we can offer back to him. That is his marvelous gift to us; we shall speak of it shortly.

At the moment, though, it is useful for us to see how generally true it is that offering comes before receiving. We must offer our willingness to love if we ever hope to be loved, although it is equally true that this willingness is awakened in us by our knowing that we *are* loved. If we hope to win friendship, we must be prepared and glad to offer our willingness to be friends. Before we can receive the cooperation of another person, we must offer our readiness to cooperate. All this is a fact of ordinary secular experience, even though frequently, if not always, the giving that is possible for us is provoked and stimulated and aided by the outgoing of another towards us. In theology we call that outgoing, when it is from God, his *prevenient grace* — the favor and strengthening that comes before and which arouses in us our desire for and our effort towards God. Yet, granted that prevenient grace, it still remains true that we must be ready and willing to give before we can get. We give because we are assured that God is "more ready to hear than we to pray, and wont to give more than either we desire or deserve."

Samuel Taylor Coleridge says in one of his poems,

> *Lady, we receive but what we give . . .*

That is true; but it is more true that what we receive is *greater* than what we give. Who could say that he had ever given enough to deserve the returning riches of life?

[26]

How far do we deserve or how can we conceivably "earn" the joy of being loved, of having friends, of the happiness of life in our family? How can we think that we "merit" the courage of our brethren in troubled times, the blessings of our social heritage, not to mention the splendor of the heavens on a winter's night or the fragrant but shy loveliness of a flower or the clean glory of a mountain peak thrust into the sky? How could we think that we deserve the devotion of others to righteousness and truth? Above all, who could say for a moment that he had given enough of himself, or could do it, to merit the cherishing love of God, which surrounds us with omnipotent charity, or the redemption wrought by Jesus Christ, or incorporation into the Body of Christ as "en-Christed" men and women, or the sharing in the divine purpose and love whereby we become "not servants but friends" of him who is the ultimate determiner of our human destiny?

Yes, we offer; but we receive in return incredibly more than we desire or deserve. And what is it that we really offer in the Eucharist?

We "plead before God," as we often say, the sacrifice of Christ for the salvation, the "wholeness," of men. Calvary is once for all; there can be no repetition of that awful but redemptive act that took place on a hill outside Jerusalem as the focal moment in the history of God's dealings with his erring human children. But if the event cannot be *repeated,* it can be *recalled.* That does not mean that it is done over again, for as we have just seen, any such thing is impossible. Yet the *value* of it, the meaning of it, the undying significance of it, can be recalled, re-presented, pleaded. This value is not in our eyes only, but deep in God himself. The total significance of Calvary, with its "benefits" or results for the world's right and true living, can be offered to God by the Body of Christ, as that Body which is the Church remembers before God what was wrought "once for all, on Calvary's tree." So the Christian can join in the hymn:

We here present, we here spread forth to thee
That only offering perfect in thine eyes,
The one true, pure, immortal sacrifice.

Throughout his history man has ever sought to find something worthy to offer to God — something that would express his adoration, his contrition for wrongs thought and said and done, his desire to love his Maker. This yearning is the explanation of all the strange and sometimes horrible sacrificial rites of primitive people, seeking in some way to find that which they might present to the god whom they worshipped. It had to be their *best* gift, even- if that meant for them the loveliest girl or the most courageous young man of the tribe, some prized animal or some other treasure. But nothing that man can offer seems, in the final count, to be worthy — save the one thing that man cannot offer, in and of his own. And what is that? It is his "soul and body, to be a reasonable, holy, and living sacrifice." Men have wanted to offer this; but their very imperfection and fault have prevented their offering it.

But that which man could never do, because all his gifts are imperfect and man himself, even at his best, is a sinner and cannot fully and utterly satisfy God's yearning, which (as man slowly comes to see) is nothing other than that he shall be his best and truest self, worthy of man and worthy of being offered to God—that which man could not do, God has done. In the humanity that the Eternal Word took upon him and shared with us in the Man Jesus Christ, God has provided a life that in its perfection is an entire offering of sheer charity to God. In and under the creaturely conditions that are ours, God indwelt and possessed a true manhood. He did this, not in spite of humankind but through a Man who at every point and in every way was responsive to the divine purpose and action. We call this the Incarnation. And on the cross that life found its full expression, its culmination. For on Calvary the offering of a human life in complete response to God was, so to say, thrown high to God the Father and thrust deep into the world of men. Now there *is* something to recall, something to remember, something to plead before God: it is the total self-giving of Jesus Christ.

However, we must not misinterpret the last paragraph. Thus to "plead Christ's passion," as summing up his entire life of self-giving to the Father, is not for the Church, or any Christian, to do in an "external" manner; it is not as if the Church pleaded Calvary *instead of* the offering of Christians themselves. What is done is done by those who have been incorporated into Christ's Body; it is done by Christ's Body into which they have been incorporated — both ways of phrasing it are true. This is the great offering in which and by which those who are thus incorporated into Christ and share in the "en-Christed" life are enabled, "made bold," to give *themselves* to God. "We show forth the Lord's death"; we "do this in remembrance" of him. In so doing, we in the Church, and the Church by us, are offered to God.

[29]

This was St. Augustine's insight when he said that on the altar is "the mystery of *yourselves*," precisely because we have been made participant in the "mystery" of Christ.

For as we have insisted, the Church *is* the Body of Christ; and it is as a fellowship in him that it worships and lives, giving itself to God so that it may be used by him for his work in the world — a work that is the ever-wider sharing with that world of the love which God *is*.

The offering of the Church, and of "every member of the same," is in union with and as part of the offering Christ himself has made to the Father. It is union with it, because the Church is the Body of him who offered himself, whose sacrifice is pleaded. It is part of it, because that which Christ did and does he wills to be shared with his people, in and through his mystical Body and not apart from its life and its work. So what the Church is really offering is that *which it is* — the Body of Christ, in union with and as part of the continual remembrance of the death and resurrection of its Lord. Its intention is that by so doing it may become in very truth more fully the Body of Christ, by receiving the life of the true Vine and conveying that life through each and every branch to the whole world.

Nor does this exhaust the meaning of the Eucharist. Here Christ is present, we believe, although the manner of his presence is a great mystery that we cannot fathom. Because he is present, his death and passion, his resurrection and ascension, are present too — for we have to do with the *whole* Christ, not with this or that particular moment in his life and work. Since Christ is present in the sacrament, in the context of his mystical Body, the Church offers itself to God, in union with and as part of the sacrifice once for all made on Calvary. But since *we*, as members of Christ's Body, are also present, we may offer ourselves to God, again in union with and as part of the offering of the Body of Christ. Here indeed is our "reasonable, holy, and living sacrifice."

Beyond that offering of ourselves, in the prayer that by this sacrament we may more fully and effectively be consecrated to God and his will, we offer also our work. Our daily tasks, our life at home, our responsibilities, our cares and our comforts, everything that we are, everything that we do, including our sinful acts repented of, such good deeds as we may have performed, all that we have and care for: all this is presented to God and offered to him for whatever use he may make of it. The typist brings here her daily load of work, the clerk his accounts, the housewife her duties with pots and pans, the school child his homework, the athlete his physical prowess, the scholar his preoccupation with research, the artist his glimpse of beauty and its translation into canvas or marble or words, the scientist his search for truth, the ditch digger his honest labor, all of us our loves and carings . . . each and every one of us brings this to God, with whatever prepares for it and follows from it, laying it down before God in union with the laying down of the life of the Son of God, to be received back renewed and transfigured because now it has been taken into the context of God's will and is part of the life of the Body of Christ, whose member each and every one of us is.

And even more is offered. The very world itself, the materiality of things, as well as history and event in that world, from dust to the *Divine Comedy*, from electron to spiral nebulae, from man's primordial gropings after the good to the struggle for righteousness that is going on in the world today: all this is offered to God, because all this is part of the world God in Christ is bringing to himself, in utter love and with redemptive passion. All this, too, is part of the mystery of the Church, in its widest and most significant sense, although to our earth-bound eyes it may not seem to be so. Here we have much to learn from our brethren in the Eastern Orthodox churches, with their stupendous faith that the entire creation, down to its lowest ranges and up to its highest points, will be returned to God as a redeemed and trans-figured thing, by the action of the same Eternal Word of God who in Jesus Christ was "enmanned" for us men. All is by the same Christ in whom, as St. Paul says, "all things consist" or cohere together, and who is also the incarnate Lord and the Head of his Church.

It is significant that in Colossians (1:14-20) St. Paul puts the two ideas right together — the cosmic sweep and the human contact — without the slightest sense of in-congruity: "All things," he says, "whether in heaven or on earth" are reconciled to God in the one Christ who is also the "Head of his Body," which is the Church. And we, as members of the Body of the same one Christ, share in the offering of the whole creation back to God through the "cosmic Christ" in whom all are being redeemed. One need hardly point out how this thought will redeem our worship from its apparent pettiness. Here there is no trace of frivolity, provincialism, or exclusivism. Everything is of Christ, for Christ, to Christ; and everything in Christ is returning to God, "to the perfection which [is possible] through him from whom it took its origin, even Jesus Christ our Lord."

We have been talking of the Divine Action here.
There is little space left to say much about the other side
of the Eucharist. But that side is more familiar to many
of us; hence it needs less stressing. There is offering or
sacrifice, in the widest sense; there is also communion
and nourishing. We give; *then we receive.* Here too is
Divine Action through our human action. Yet how much
more do we receive than give! We "offer ourselves, our
souls and bodies," as "very members incorporate in the
mystical Body of Christ which is the blessed company of
all faithful people." We present our world to God, our
work and all that we have and hope for. We receive back
from God "our selves, our souls and bodies," now given
a new dignity and sharing a new life because they are
now actually "in Christ." We receive back, as the Church,
the true meaning and life of the Church as Body of
Christ, now instinct with his Spirit and vivified anew by
his divine life brought to us in sacramental sharing. We
receive back the whole world, and our work in it, now
transfigured and changed because known and seen in a
new context, in the redeemed creation of God, sharing
with us in that consummation for which "the earnest
expectation of the creation" at this very moment "groan-
eth and travaileth," awaiting its "redemption, namely
the revealing of the sons of God."

But most obviously we receive back from God the
bread and the wine we have offered to him for his use.
They *were* the tokens of our oblation, in union with
Christ. <u>*Now,* through the action of the Holy Spirit, they
have become the tokens of Christ himself.</u> They are his
tokens, not by merely symbolizing his presence with us
and his giving himself to us in some superficial or acci-

[33]

dental fashion, but by becoming the instrumental means by which that presence, really and genuinely, effectually and certainly, is made known to us, and that giving of himself to us is achieved.

> *Faith our outward sense befriending*
> *Makes the inward vision clear . . .*

and we see and know "the bread which came down from heaven" and the blood that was poured out on Calvary for our redemption. We have with us now "him who pleads above," as the hymn puts it. In, through, with, and under our gifts of bread and wine, the true life of Jesus Christ, our Lord and Saviour, comes to us, dwells with us, nourishes us, at the table that is his holy banqueting table. We are fed with the life of him who is our Life.

So it is that the Body of Christ characteristically expresses itself. In the Eucharist, where a Divine Action occurs in what to those who do not have the eye of faith is *merely* a human action, we have instead a human action that by God's blessing *is* a Divine Action. This is the heart and center of Christianity, from which everything else flows and to which it must unfailingly return. Thanks be to God, we may well say, for this his unspeakable gift.

3

The Priesthood of the People of God

The meaning of priesthood, in Christian terms, is probably more misunderstood and misrepresented than any other single idea held by the Christian Church in respect to the significance of ministry. It is therefore important, in our thinking about the Body of Christ and the Eucharist as the characteristic Christian action, to endeavor to clear up this matter. We need a sound and right conception of priesthood, based on biblical teaching; we need a conception that can stand up to critical attack. For no matter how badly the notion of priesthood has been misinterpreted in many quarters, there can be no doubt that it has been central in the Christian tradition and particularly relevant to the celebration of the Eucharist.

The first point that should be grasped is the order of significance and derivation in the priesthood of the minister of the Christian Church. Here we can begin with a flat statement nobody should question: the only underived and undelegated priesthood about which a Christian may speak is the priesthood of Jesus Christ himself. In Christian faith, there is a coincidence in Jesus of divine activity and human activity; traditionally this has been stated by the phrase "God-man," or by talk

about his divinity and humanity. But however we may
wish to express it in terms of formal christology, the fact
remains that in Jesus Christ Christian faith discerns the
reality of true and genuine manhood and at the same
time a particular and special operation of God. Because
this is the case, Jesus Christ can be and is representative
of God to man and of man to God. He is himself the
mediator, and the only adequate mediator, between God
and man. This is because in him the two terms that are
mediated are present in the highest degree. Thus he is
the great High Priest.

A priest, according to dictionary definition and proper
usage, is one who does thus mediate between God and
man. But if there is in Jesus Christ such a relationship
of the two as Christian conviction affirms, there is in
consequence mediation in its complete reality. His is the
originative priesthood. But it is not a priesthood that he
allows to be restricted to himself alone. For the priesthood of Christ is effectually present in the priesthood
we attribute to the Church as a whole. It is the Body of
the living Christ; it is part of the very life of Christ.
Hence it shares with its Head and its Lord whatever is
proper to him. The Church is not alien to Christ, nor
is it incidental to his life and purpose. It is integral to
him; it is his continuing way of being with his world.
Thus it shares in that which is Christ's. It shares in his
priesthood. The priesthood Christ is willing to share
with his Body is his own priesthood — it is not some
derivative or delegated priesthood, but the true and
genuine and full priesthood that is Christ's own. In
I Peter, we read of the Church as "a royal priesthood";
and that means that it is the priesthood of Christ who

is the *King*. Our Lord's kingship is not after the fashion of earthly rulers, with the worldly majesty and the pomp and display we associate with such. It is a suffering kingship, seen most vividly when he is crowned with thorns and hanging on the cross; nonetheless it is royalty in its divine truth. The kingship of Christ is found in perfect service. As St. Augustine said, "to serve *is* to reign." Thus the royal priesthood of Christ, shared in the royal priesthood of which St. Peter speaks when he writes about the Body of Christ, is also a priesthood of service — and to that we shall return.

Yet when we speak of the priesthood of Christ, shared in the priesthood proper to the Church, we have not come to a full stop. For the Body of Christ has its *members,* who are so participant in its ongoing life that whatever is true of the Body as a whole is also true, in its mode and degree, of each and every member of the Body. Thereby we are brought to see that all members of the Church, members of Christ's Body, are by that token made sharers in Christ's priesthood extended and known in the Church. Hence the doctrine of the priesthood of the laity, which we may rightly call "the priesthood of all believers," is an integral and essential part of the picture.

This priesthood, belonging to each of us who is a Christian, is not ours simply by virtue of the individual relationship we sustain with our Lord and Saviour. We do in truth have such a relationship; but the priestly quality of the Christian life is derived from participation in the Body of Christ. It is not an individualistic doctrine, although some who have defended its importance may have talked about it in that fashion. It is ours because we are "Church-men." Nor is there, as some have thought, an "uncatholic" ring about the "priesthood of all believers"; it is a doctrine as old as the New Testament and as old as the Church itself. The reason that it has appeared to many to be peculiarly a "Reformation" doctrine is simply that the Reformers asserted it with particular vehemence, since it had been overlooked in the period before the Reformation and needed reemphasis. We may also admit that in their eagerness some of the Reformers sometimes asserted it without due regard for the Church setting of the "priesthood" of every Christian man; they sometimes made it appear as a man's possession in too individualistic a way, rather than through his belonging to the people of God, the "laity" or *laos* that includes *all* who are members of the Body of Christ.

"Catholic" Christians are also accustomed to speak of the particular priesthood of the ordained ministry of the Church. All "Catholic" Christians would be zealous for and jealous of the conviction that their clergyman is not merely one who acts on behalf of the local congregation as their chosen delegate; they would agree that the minister is to speak with a prophetic voice but they would insist that he is not the only one who is to speak in this manner. In a genuine sense, they would say, an ordained minister is a priest. But once this is said, we need to be sure that we understand exactly what is meant. No Christian could mean that the minister is a priest in a sense that makes him a substitute for Christ's priesthood, nor for that of the Body of Christ, which is the Church, nor for the "priesthood of the laity" or "of all believers." To think in that way would be unscriptural, uncatholic in the best meaning of that word, and a blasphemous denial of what the Scots Presbyterians have styled "the crown rights of Jesus Christ."

What is intended here is something quite different. For the kind of "priesthood" that, as we may rightly maintain, is indeed conferred upon the ordained minister is a delegated, a representative, and a functional priesthood; it is not *his own,* to be accepted with personal pride. In the famous phrase of R. C. Moberly, it is a "ministerial priesthood." That means that it is the priesthood of Christ in his priestly Body, shared with all his members, but functioning through the instrumentality of a particular man who has been designated for the purpose by the Church, after due examination and the certainty that he has been "called" to this office and work. In everything that the ministerial priest may do, he is acting only and solely for Christ in his Church, on behalf of and for Christ's people, towards the world which Christ loves. Here all Christian denominations are finding a point of agreement.

Thus to speak of "his" priesthood is or ought to be impossible for any ordained minister, since it is always Christ's priesthood in his Church that has the priority. If for convenience' sake we call the ordained man "priest," we must do it with the adjectives "delegated, designated, functional, instrumental, representative, ministerial" taken for granted and intended always to be understood.

Nor does ministerial priesthood call into question any of the offices that traditionally the Church intends the minister to perform; on the contrary, it gives them their special sanction. *All* priesthood devolves from above, in the sense that it is from Christ, through his Body, among the priestly people, that it has its origin. It comes from

[39]

Christ in his Church to the particular man who has been "called," chosen, and ordained to act for Christ's Church, in the celebration of the sacraments, the preaching of the faith, the shepherding of the people, the proclamation of the divine purpose, and the serving of men in charity, with courage and humility. This certainly is the primitive and true Catholic conception of the priesthood. If it were more widely understood, with its background and context explained, all Christian groups would be ready to welcome this ancient and Christian view of ministry — as indeed they are coming to do, of themselves, as both theologians and lay people try to see what ordained ministry really signifies.

The specific *word* that we may choose to describe this ministering function is not very important. If "presbyter" will serve, let it be employed. But "priest" is a traditional term and it carries *many* of the right associations, although it can also suggest entirely *wrong* notions — and certainly it has done both in the course of Christian history. But the mediation between God and man remains, whatever the word used, provided we always insist on the derivative nature of the ordained minister's mediating role. And the function of mediation has historically been linked with that of priesthood.

The function of the ordained minister is thus to mediate between God and man, not instead of, over against, or unrelated to the priestly quality of every Christian's life, which is also mediatorial; above all, not as if he were doing once again what Jesus Christ did once for all. The minister's work is on behalf of, acting for, and in the name of that Lord; and it is also on

[40]

behalf of, acting for, and in the name of the priestly Body with all its priestly members.

Man has always yearned for a relationship between God and himself in which there may be a free and open intercourse between them. To secure this, he has made his offerings to God. He has held meals of sacrificial communion in which such a union was, he thought, realized. He has appointed men with special duties to act for him in this mediatorial role. All these elements, and much else, in primitive religion find their fulfillment and correction in the person and work of Jesus Christ. He offers himself to God to secure union between God and man; he offers himself to men so that they may be enabled to enjoy, through him, communion with God. He acts for men and he acts for God by virtue of his place as that One in whom God and man are so intimately, directly, and truly brought into union. Nothing is needed to make the mediation more "perfect"; it is already and forever "the full, perfect, and sufficient" mediation between God and man. Into it others are to enter, as they are incorporated into his Body and live his life.

The difference between Jesus Christ the High Priest and a man who has been ordained to the ministerial priesthood by the Church is one thing. The difference between the priesthood of Christ and the supposed "priesthood" of one appointed to serve in a primitive or non-Christian cult is another. In the latter case the designation is from man's side, while in the former (according to Christian faith) Jesus Christ was appointed by God himself to be the mediator between God and man. The Epistle to the Hebrews stresses this singularity of Christ's priesthood. He has been "set forth," "appointed," or sent by God to exercise this function of mediator. Through his uniting in himself the human nature that is ours with the divine activity or nature, he speaks and acts for God as well as for men. In Hebrews, the stress is on both the similarity and the difference between the priestly conception found in Jewish religious thought and the Christian priesthood established in Christ as the Lord of the Church. We shall do well to pattern our own thinking after that of the unknown author of this very early Christian tractate.

Now it is in the liturgy, the Eucharist, that the priestly work of Christ is "remembered" and continued, although that act of worship is set in the context of a wider mediatorial life and work in the world. The liturgy, as we have insisted, is the characteristically Christian thing; and it is Christ's own action in his Body. Much else in Christian thought is illuminated when this centrality of the Eucharist is seen for what it is. The theology of the Eucharist helps us to understand — to take but one example — what the doctrine of the Atonement intends. Failure to take account of the eucharistic associations of the Atonement can produce a mechanical view of how Christ redeems mankind. But the language we use at the Holy Communion makes very clear these associations. Take, for example, from one of the Anglican prayers of consecration, the important opening words: "All glory be to thee, Almighty God our heavenly Father, for that thou of thy tender mercy didst give thine only Son Jesus Christ to suffer death upon the cross for our redemption; who made there, by his one oblation of himself once offered, a full, perfect, and sufficient sacrifice, oblation, and satisfaction for the sins of the whole world; and did institute, and in his holy gospel command us to continue, a perpetual memory of this his precious death and sacrifice, until his coming again. For in the night in which he was betrayed, he took bread. . . ."

Similarly in the Series II communion service of the Church of England, the prayer of consecration states exactly the same connection. It is put plainly and unequivocally. The Divine Action on Calvary, which is the means for the redemption of mankind, is made available to God's children through the human action of eucharistic worship. In that action, "recalling" Calvary and feeding on the bread and wine, which are the sacramental instruments effectively nourishing men with Christ's living presence, the "benefits" of God's deed are shared with men. Thus the Divine Action of Christ on Calvary *is* the Divine Action of Christ in his mystical Body. In the Eucharist God and man are brought into union one with another, for it is in that eucharistic rite that Calvary is remembered or re-presented in a humanly performed action, and God and man are made one in the person of Christ himself who comes to dwell in his people. Thus we both enter into and plead before God the Father the already accomplished union of the Godhead and manhood, as at the holy table we offer "this our sacrifice of praise and thanksgiving" and receive into ourselves the life of the risen Lord.

So the Church as Body of Christ is priestly, mediating God to man and man to God, in the power and through the presence of him who is the Mediator. Each member of the Church, by virtue of his baptismal incorporation, shares in the priesthood of the Church. Some men are designated to represent this priesthood in ministering work for Christ in his Body. This is the proper conception and this is the right ordering of priesthood; it is primitive and scriptural in background, it is truly evangelical and truly Catholic, and it makes sense to us today.

Up to this point we have been speaking of priesthood in its "man to God" sense. But priesthood is not only towards God; it is also towards *men*. Our great High Priest Jesus Christ was the Priest of God to every man, mediating the divine reality in every moment, in every action, in every word, in all that he did and said and was. In his Church he is still doing the same. The Gospels tell us, as Acts puts it, what "Jesus *began* to do and to teach." The continuation of that doing and teaching is the history of the Christian Church up to this present moment, as Jesus unfailingly brings God to men. He makes them members of his Body, he gives to them the life that is his own, and he unites men to God in that Body and by that life. This is a side of priesthood that frequently is forgotten in Christian theology; yet it is just as real and important as the other side of priesthood.

We are ever ready to remember Christ as our Priest to God. We think readily enough of the Church as a priestly community bringing us, and in the end all men, into union through Christ with our heavenly Father. We may forget, however, that the Church's priesthood, like the originative priesthood of its Head, is also towards and for men. To bring the love and care of God to every son of man; to see that men are assured of God's forgiveness, nourished by his goodness, challenged by his holy will, and empowered through his grace to obey it: this too is part of the priesthood of the Church. And

[44]

this is part of that shared priesthood which attaches to every member of the Church who has been made a sharer in the life of the mystical Body of Christ.

There are the specified and regular ways in which, through Christian history, the ordained minister carries out this task. The feeding of the faithful with the life of Christ in Holy Communion; the forgiving of sins, whether by public declaration in the course of a service of worship or in the privacy of the sacramental rite of confession and absolution; the blessing of men and women in any and every circumstance and above all in the highly significant moments of their lives; the proclamation of the Word of Truth and the teaching of the Christian life to children and adults; the prophetic denunciation of sin and wickedness by men in their public and private behavior — all this is done by the man who has been ordained to speak and act for God. This we know and accept. But it is not so often remembered by laymen and laywomen that each of them, too, in these matters and in many others, has his own personal responsibility precisely because he is possessed of a priestly character.

Thus every Christian, sharing as he does in Christ's priesthood, is intended to be an agent who will bring to the world the nourishing life of Christ, the sovereign blessing of Christ, the forgiving love of Christ, his clear call to public and private righteousness, his truth that redeems life from futility, and his grace that surrounds life with divine power. This is not best done through the layman's taking upon himself the specific functions that have been delegated to the minister. There is a principle of "ordering" in the Body of Christ; every man

[45]

is to fulfill "*his* office and ministry," not that of some-body else. But it is to be done, nonetheless; and the ways of doing it every Christian must discover for him-self. The ways are particular for this man and that man, where in his own time and place opportunities are offered to make his witness and perform his work. So he can "truly and godly" serve the brethren, for his Lord, as a "living member" of the Body of Christ.

Furthermore, all this finds its symbolic expression when the Christian is present at the eucharistic celebra-tion. When the Church offers its "sacrifice of praise and thanksgiving," recalling Christ's life and achievement, and receiving his "benefits," all Christians are in prin-ciple present and ought to be present in fact. That is part of their sharing in priesthood. The priesthood that is ours does not stop there, however. It is to be taken out into the world and manifested in that world, in its lanes and highways, its shops and homes, its factories and offices and schools. The member of Christ, because he is a branch of the true Vine, is to bring forth in his daily life the "fruits of his redemption." For to him belongs a participation in the priesthood of incarnate God himself.

That incarnate Lord "entered not into the holy places made with hands, which are the figures of the true, but into heaven itself, now to appear in the presence of God for us." By that act of high priesthood, he "offered him-self through the eternal Spirit without spot to God." And to what end? That we, his members, should have "our conscience purged from dead works to serve the living God."

[46]

4
The Eucharist and the Christian Man

If one asked the average man what it means to be a Christian, he would doubtless reply, "Doing good things." He is not entirely wrong, of course; but there is something more basic than that, something that is specifically a matter of faith and more profoundly a matter of life. It is with this that we shall be concerned more than fulfillment of moral obligation; it should indicate that the Christian man is marked by certain qualities, that he is a specific sort of person who, precisely because he is this, will feel *impelled* to "do good things."

Otherwise we are likely to find ourselves in the position so amusingly described by George Tyrrell, whom we have already quoted in a different connection. Tyrrell said that there are altogether too many people for whom Christianity consists in "going about doing good," particularly the kind of "doing good" that involves a great deal of "going about."

The real answer to the question, "What does it mean to be a Christian?" is that it means being an "en-Christed man." It means to live "in Christ," to have one's existence on the level of that God-man relationship established in Jesus Christ, and to have that stance as the

[47]

point from which all else springs. Thus, to be a Christian is another way of saying that one is in and of the Body of Christ, where the "en-Christed life" is known and shared. It is another way of saying that one realizes, as fully as one can, and in one's own way and to one's own proper degree, the richness of membership in the Body, the wonder of being a branch of the true Vine.

Because one is thus incorporated into the Body of Christ, one accepts the basic affirmations of the faith that gives significance to the life of the Body. One participates with due regularity in the Divine Action of the Body, the Eucharist, where, in union with and as a part of the self-oblation of Christ in his Church, the Christian offers himself, his soul and body, to God, and in return receives the bread from heaven and the wine of God's all-encompassing love. As the earlier chapters of this book argued, the Christian has entered into his priesthood as a member of the Body of Christ the great High Priest; he brings the world to God in total donation and he brings God to the world in generous outward-moving love. To sum up what has been urged, the Christian is himself a *liturgy* — that is, as the Greek word *leitourgia* would show, a publicly manifest expression of God in Christ to the world. Or to put it in more readily understandable words, the Christian is a *liturgical man,* whose whole being is formed by and informed with the spirit of the Church's liturgy.

Any conception of the Christian man that is less than this, or different from this, is hardly adequate to the picture the Christian Church historically has intended to paint and consistently wished to teach. In this respect, we must admit that a very considerable part of our

[48]

modern understanding of the significance of Christian profession has been a *mis*understanding. Either a different conception has been presented — as, for example, that a Christian is somebody who believes certain things, and that is all — or the part has been taken for the whole — as in that business of "doing good" — or (worst of all) an entirely erroneous view has been communicated — as when it appears that to be a Christian means only to be a "decent citizen." None of these examples is *entirely* false, of course. There is nothing wrong with believing certain things, if they happen to be true; there is most certainly a demand that a Christian shall do good; and there is every reason to hope that the Christian will be a good citizen, insofar as his good citizenship is not in conflict with his Christian profession. But unless all these things are seen in the context of the "en-Christed life," with its liturgical grounding, they are so partial that they can give a very mistaken impression.

But how does one become the liturgical man? Surely not so much by striving and struggling in a moral fashion towards some supposed perfection; rather, the man who is formed by and informed with the spirit of the liturgy comes to that specifically Christian mode of existence by continuing exposure to God and to God's activity as these are made available to him through his participation in the Divine Action that in its humanly conditioned expression is *the* liturgy. By the deepest possible sharing in this continuing work of the Church, there may be developed in us such a close attachment to the Body of Christ that we become, as used to be said in France, "des autres Christs" — "other Christs" in the power and by the indwelling presence of Christ our

[49]

Lord himself. A Christian, said Martin Luther and *also* St. Benedict, is to be "a Christ" to his brethren. From that, there follows a deepening of the social sense of our faith, as well as an ever richer appreciation of the total sacramental relationship with God and men that is ours. From that sharing too there comes a more profound grasp of the truths of the Christian faith itself. What that faith has to say about God, his way and will, his self-disclosure, comes alive in the liturgical participant. And finally, from that sharing there develops a life in outward action that exerts a social influence that can be both pervasive and persuasive.

The point we are trying to make is that by our full attachment to the Church, taking our proper part in its living work of worship, we enter into and appropriate the fact of our relationship as members of the Body and branches of the true Vine. This is hard to accept for many people today, simply because they see the Church merely in its institutional aspect and rightly regard this as less than perfect. They look at its ecclesiastical house-keeping, the pettiness and absurdity of so much that goes on within the institution, the failure of Christians to live up to their profession; they are bored by un-imaginative conduct of worship and dull and irrelevant sermons. Nobody could deny that a good deal of what one sees *is* hardly appealing. Yet insight ought to help such people to discern the deeper reality, so frequently obscured if not hidden by the *externalia* that seem so unpleasant. Nor is there much to be said for the attitude of those who simply "contract out" of the institutional Church on these grounds. By doing that, they are only making matters worse. What is required of us all, but

[50]

what is more particularly required of the critical person, is an ever more faithful participation, through which he may make his contribution towards the realization, by the institution and by its membership, of the *reality* here present. As William Temple said, in words already quoted, "Let the Church *be* the Church" — and it is incumbent upon us all to do everything in our power to make that come true in our own time, our own place, and our own lives.

Those who do thus try to enter more deeply into the Church's reality will find that as time passes they discover much more than they had at first thought was there. As they use more faithfully and regularly the appointed ways of Christian worship, they find that the Church has provided for them, at every moment and in every range of experience, the possibility of an intimate comradeship with God, who is all-surrounding and all-cherishing of his human children. Thus the truths upon which Christian life is based will be known more fully, more intimately, and more compellingly; they will become part of a man's living experience rather than mere formulas he simply accepts on the say-so of somebody else. In consequence of this continuing process of liturgical participation, he will become increasingly a healthy, life-giving cell of the Body, exerting an influence upon the world that doubtless will be largely unknown to himself but will be quite apparent to those with whom he happens to have contacts. In the words used of the first Christian disciples, men will "take notice" that this contemporary Christian has "been with Jesus."

Some of us would confess that we are "radical" Christians, concerned to work out a "new theology," very

[51]

uneasy about institutionalism, troubled by the lack of vitality in Christian circles, unhappy about merely formal worship, distressed by the failure of professed Christians to implement their profession in their daily activity. The danger is that such "radicals," including the writer of this book, will so concentrate on *these* matters, important as they are, that they will not devote much of their time and thought to a consideration of the enormous *privilege* of membership in Christ's Church. They will perhaps lack charity towards many a "church-mouse" who for one reason or another does not show the imaginative grasp of the Christian "thing" that is so desirable. Hence they will fail to see that in all probability that "church-mouse" is a much more faithful servant of the Lord than they themselves could dare to claim. A certain humility is required of those who very properly are anxious to work for the renewal of the Church, for a radical revision of its formularies, and for a more zealous expression in ordinary affairs of the Christian attitude and spirit.

All of us, without exception, need to meditate gratefully on the fact of our having been incorporated into Christ's mystical Body. We need to be thankful for the privilege of having been made, through Baptism, "en-Christed" men and women. Our responsibility is not to struggle after some far distant and perhaps almost unattainable ideal; it is to realize (in the sense of "making real to ourselves"), so much as in us lies and by the help of God's grace, what is in truth a given, present fact — the fact of our "en-Christed" membership in Jesus Christ. Martin Luther, when troubled by controversy and disturbed by his own failure, used to say to himself,

"I have been baptized." How right and sound was that practice! For our having been made members of Christ, which is what happens in Baptism, has put us on the right path to true human fulfillment; our task now is to walk in that path, confident that the grace of God in Jesus Christ will always be available to us as we seek to move forward.

If, in our attempts to lead what we often call "a better life," we think of the virtues of faith, hope, and love as if they were far off and remote, like distant stars we faintly hope to reach, we are defeated from the start. But if we think of those virtues as the right habits of behavior, the right attitudes of mind and will, which are slowly made alive in us as we live together in the fellowship of other believers, as members of the Body of Christ, we shall much more probably come nearer to living Christianly in this world. The supposed remoteness and intangibility of far-off "ideals" may make them seem like a will-o'-the-wisp. But the gradual growth of good habits, the formation of a new self, will come to us through never ceasing exposure to the love of God as we experience it in eucharistic worship and enter wholeheartedly in the life of fellowship with the brethren. Christ will be "formed in us"; we shall become more fully the "en-Christed" persons we are intended to be.

There is place for discipline in the Christian life. Nobody who has sought to realize his profession would deny that for a moment. Yet it is equally true that frequently a relaxation of effort, with a substitution for such effort of simple basking in God's loving presence in Christ and a simple willingness to be with our fellow

Christians in adoration and worship and work, will do the job more effectively.

Furthermore, we should remember how grateful, as well as humble, we must be for membership in the mystical Body of Christ. The great majority of Christian people seem simply to take it for granted; they do not have anything like a sufficient spirit of thankfulness for what they have been given. They do not consider seriously the dignity of their Christian belonging. A wise old parson used to say to his people time and time again, "Thank God every day that you have been baptized; thank him that you have been confirmed; thank him that you can come to the Holy Communion. If you would stop worrying about your failures all the time, and now and again just be glad that you are what by God's grace you are — a Christian, a member of Christ's Church, even if a pretty poor specimen — you would get farther along the road to real Christian discipleship."

How truly and deeply that minister saw into the heart of Christianity! In word, we are prepared to say that to be a Christian, to share in what we have been styling the "en-Christed life," to be baptized into the mystical Body of Christ, is so important that we want to have our children baptized at the earliest possible age, lest they miss some of the influences and helps Baptism will bring them. And then we ourselves make almost nothing of the fact of membership, once it is established! There is a strange sort of inverted selfishness and self-concern in the way in which we are prepared to make the most of our own shortcomings, forgetting or neglecting to stress the sheer fact of the "churchly appurtenance," as Baron von Hügel was accustomed to describe it, in which, through no merit of our own, we have been permitted to share.

The Christian man is one whose life is being shaped by the liturgy of the Body of Christ. That liturgy, supremely in its eucharistic expression, is the informing principle in his human existence. His outward life, like his innermost thought, comes to be a reflection of this central principle. Inevitably and inescapably, once he permits himself to be molded by and built up in the liturgical life of the Church, his whole being becomes "liturgical." In recent years, few books have so admirably presented this process as the Clare College talks given by J. A. T. Robinson and published under the title *Liturgy Comes to Life*. One particular value of those talks is that they indicate clearly what will be discussed later in this book: that the forming of the Christian man by his liturgical experience is the indispensable preliminary for the external expression, in daily life, of what Christian faith is all about.

One way in which growth in liturgical awareness will express itself is in a more profound grounding of personal faith in the wide context of corporate Christian belief. Historically the Christian tradition has worked out its faith in the form of dogmatic statements. These are the accepted and agreed beliefs of Christian people, we like to say. But such affirmations are given vitality when we are nourished and supported by the life in grace the liturgy provides for us. And in particular we are delivered by the liturgy from a too selective attitude towards the rounded tradition of belief. The readings or lections, covering as they do the whole range of faith, secure a well-rounded and proportionate entrance into what that faith declares. Thus there is less of the fussy "picking and choosing" that leads us to concentrate all our attention on, say, man's sin while forgetting God's redemption, or on the death of Christ on Good Friday with no regard for his victorious conquest of death in the Easter triumph. Instead, the liturgical man experiences what may be a slow or gradual, but will certainly be a greatly enriching, conforming of his personal grasp of Christian faith to the ongoing community's apprehension of that faith. On Christmas, God's humility in entering so fully into human life, for our true human living, will be in his mind; at Easter, the victory of God in human life over the forces of sin and evil and death will be brought before him. When Whitsunday comes around, the empowering gift of the Holy Spirit enabling men to respond to God will receive his attention. On All Saints', he will think of the holy ones of God and the example they set for him to follow. On Passion Sunday, he will recognize the awful tragedy of human sin and the willingness of God to act for its forgiveness. Good Friday will explicitly present to him what God did, in that act, for man's forgiveness. Thus, listed without proper sequence in the preceding sentences but in the "Christian year" arranged carefully and systematically, the wholeness of faith is provided and an opportunity is given to follow through, with sanity and breadth, "the mystery of our creation and redemption."

We have mentioned the lections or readings that form part of the liturgy. Doubtless there might be and will be improvement in the selections from Holy Scripture that are found in the "calendars" for the various daily services and for the celebration of the Eucharist. But even

as they stand in most of the lists provided by the several
churches, they are the result of long thought and careful
selection. One could say that any man who based his
religious life on the appointed lections in the Eucharist
alone, for example as now given in the Anglican Prayer
Books, would not miss much of the basic content of
what is called "biblical theology." Thus the person who
follows the liturgy is enabled to grasp the origins of his
faith and is helped to make the same response the men
and women of an earlier day made to the action of God
in human affairs.

When it comes to the "good works" a Christian is
meant to "walk in" (to employ again phrases from the
old Prayer of Thanksgiving in the Church of England
1662 Prayer Book), we can see that the *intent* of the
liturgy is eminently practical. It is concerned with the
reality of worship and with the truths of faith, but it
always leads out into Christian behavior. It may be desirable but it is hardly necessary to use, at the end of a
service of worship, the conventional prayer that "what
we believe in our hearts we may practice in our lives."
The entire liturgy, and supremely the Eucharist, is concerned to make that point clear as day. The very words
make plain that worship and work go together. Anybody
who hears those words knows that while activity without
worship can be meaningless, worship that does not
result in Christian action is sterile.

The Church's liturgical action, then, is designed to
help us to become Christians; it is intent upon making
us Christian men and women. We are "formed by the
liturgy," so that as Christians we may act *like* Christians.
Before outward expression and social action, there must

[57]

be personal appropriation and true participation in the "en-Christed life." We must become Christian people before we can hope to act like Christian people. Towards the making of such people the liturgical action of the Church plays its essential part. It imbues the whole of our personality, soul and body — both of which are concerned with and have a share in that worship — with the Spirit of Christ.

So we may say that the point of worship is both to direct us to God in Christ, notably through the Eucharist, and also to help us to bring into full expression, in every range of our being, what we *are*: "en-Christed" men and women, branches of the true Vine, members of the one Body, sharers in the life of God in Christ.

5
The Eucharist and Social Awareness

Archbishop William Temple once described the "individualistic" Christian as one who says, "I believe in one holy infallible Church, of which I regret to say that at the present time I am the only member." And the distinguished English economist R. H. Tawney, who was also a devout Christian, said in an oft-quoted remark that "the man who seeks God in isolation from his fellows is likely to find, not God, but the devil, who will bear an embarrassing resemblance to himself."

These two comments help us to see what is wrong with the man or woman who somehow assumes that he can be a Christian apart from *other* men and women. Perhaps very few people today would wish to defend such an extremely individualistic conception of Christian faith, turning it into a matter of "each man for himself." Most of us have come to see that whatever else Christianity may be, it most certainly is a corporate reality, a shared experience, a socially conveyed and socially apprehended religious tradition, which requires of each of us some genuine willingness to sink our personal prejudices and preferences in a common cause and to be keenly aware of the others with whom we live and work. This does not suggest, of course, that we try to destroy our good and God-given personality or whatever may have been granted us in personal insight and understanding. But it does mean that whatever may be ours personally is likely to be enriched by the experience of sharing together in a community. Furthermore, it indicates that we are at least conscious of the fact that personal idiosyncrasies may mar our apprehension and that the common life may help us to broaden our vision and enlarge our capacity to grasp the realities of faith.

But while very few people today would be prepared to *defend* individualistic Christianity, a great many people do, as a matter of fact, live as if they were able to get along reasonably well without their Christian brethren. Frequently we hear talk about *"my* religion," as if the faith were something we had worked out for ourselves; we hear people speak of *"my* idea of God," as if they were prepared to think that their notion of things was the sole determiner of the truth. We hear criticisms of the Church, its services of worship, its faith, its ministers, merely on the ground that they are not congruous with "my" particular ideas of what they ought to be. There are plenty of people who refuse to have anything to do with the institutional Church, or decline to support its work or to take part in its worship, on the excuse that these fail in certain ways to please "me" or that they are exercised or conducted in a fashion that offends "me."

Now we have already admitted, in the preceding chapters, that there is much in institutional Christianity and in the organized Christian Church that is imperfect and in need of radical reform. But to admit that fact

[60]

is very different from refusing all cooperation with, participation in, and support of the Church as it stands. In most of the instances we have just mentioned, we can be sure that at bottom there is not so much a justifiable concern for necessary reform and a distress at Christian failure in the institution, as there is an individualistic notion of Christianity itself — and individualism in religious faith is *wrong*. Alfred North Whitehead once defined religion as what a man "does with his solitariness"; his definition has been seriously misused to suggest that Whitehead was defending religious "individualism." He was not, as the context of his remark in *Religion in the Making* clearly shows. The emphasis falls on the verb "does": what is *done* about and with that "solitariness" which is part of human existence, that inescapable privacy which makes each man a self. Hence we may very well say that one type of man does one sort of thing, another type of man another, in respect to that selfhood. One type refuses to relate his selfhood to the deep sociality of which he is part, willy-nilly, and attempts to "go it alone." The other type gladly relates himself to his fellows because he knows that in and of himself, in supposed isolation, he will never come to any richness of religious life and experience. The critic of the Church who sets up to have everything his own way is an unattractive figure; we appreciate much more the man who is willing and able to give up some of his personal fancies in order to cooperate in a good and great cause.

Within the Church there are people who tacitly accept, while they inwardly reject, the impact of the Christian faith simply because there are some "items" in the traditional scheme they dislike — perhaps dislike with justice.

There are people who despite their keen activity in church affairs are yet much more intent on "teaching the Church" than "being taught of the Church." What we mean here is that such persons simply will not *listen* to the accumulated wisdom of the Christian ages. There may be, and many of us are convinced that there are, real and necessary adjustments required in the Church's statement of its faith; there are important problems that need careful examination and reverent but fearless handling. But to reject the main drive or thrust of Christian faith simply because one does not like some of the ways in which the total thing has been taught, or because there are aspects or elements that need radical revision, is rather like declining to continue to be a loyal subject of the Queen because one dislikes some of those who share in government or certain laws that may have been passed by Parliament. One can always assent to the whole, even when one is not in full agreement with the particular ways in which some particular detail is stated or even when one feels that this or that detail is an obstacle — an unnecessary and perhaps serious obstacle — to the best and truest meaning of the whole.

It is even possible to find persons who conform to the Church's liturgy, to the Divine Action in human action that is the Eucharist, but who are not willing to be "formed by" the liturgy so that they may enter into the social and corporate life of the fellowship. Yet anyone who enters at all earnestly and sympathetically into the liturgical life of the Church will discover there unsuspected riches, while he may also have some of his own narrowness and prejudice removed. Indeed, there is no more effective way of learning that nobody is a Christian in and of himself than by thus entering earnestly and sympathetically into the worship of the Christian fellowship. For the liturgy of the Church from start to finish is a social matter; and since it is the characteristic action of the Christian Church, that indicates plainly that Christianity is a social religion.

Looking at the Gospels, we can see that the principle "every man for himself" has no place in the picture of discipleship given by our Lord Jesus Christ. If there is anything that is clear from the Gospel record of Jesus' teaching, it is that he declared that all men are brethren, children of a common Father, to whom, when they pray, they say "*Our* Father." In Jesus' teaching, all men are to share generously and gladly with one another, entering into the situations in which their brethren find themselves, urgent in the desire to help them to the uttermost, sharing in the family life under God as Father and with all men as children of that Father who is God.

This insistence that we are "members one of another," as St. Paul put it, is placarded before us in the liturgical action of the Church. It is impossible to engage in the Eucharist without some glimpse of this truth, even if we do not implement this truth in our life and thought. No individual can enter heart and soul into liturgical prayer and *remain* simply an individual; he cannot fail to see, nor can he avoid some slight growth in, the sociality of Christian faith. Of course he cannot — but then too many of us do not thus enter "heart and soul"; we enter with our "mind" alone, to criticize, or with our "body" alone, to go through the outward motions of conformity.

Consider the Eucharist. Its words of prayer are entirely in the plural. It is "our" sacrifice; it is "we" who

[63]

"celebrate and make" it; it is Christ's dwelling in "us" and "we" in him. Nor is this use of the plural just a matter of liturgical convenience; it is a matter of liturgical *principle*. It is also a matter of Christian faith, for Christianity is a "we" religion. Naturally and inevitably there must be the personal acceptance and the personal application of the salvation wrought for men in Christ, the personal feeding of the soul by Christ's life. Hence the singular pronoun is used in the words of administration of the elements in the Holy Communion: "for *thee*." When men accept the truth or when they receive nourishment, they must do it each for himself. Yet they do it as members of a family; they do it, being Christians, as members of Christ's Body. "I" am still very important; but it is "I" as one of God's children in his family, "I" as one of the members of Christ's mystical Body.

When we assist at the Eucharist in the recalling before God of Christ's "saving passion, his resurrection from the dead, and his glorious ascension into heaven," in the words of the Series II Communion Service in the Church of England, "looking for the coming of his kingdom," it is "we" who pray God "to accept this our duty and service," and ask that "*we* may so eat and drink these holy things in the presence of thy divine majesty, that *we* may be filled with thy grace and heavenly blessing." So we are taking part and finding our place in a great company. We stand together; we kneel together; we bow together. If we pray at all, we pray together. We sing hymns; we repeat creed and confession; we join with our brethren to "offer and present" ourselves to God. There is no room here for "everyone for himself"; it is "each for all, and all for Christ." Our little individual idiosyncrasies, our peculiar personal prejudices, our personal tastes and dislikes are washed clean of all self-centeredness in the total life of the Body of Christ. We enter into and make our own, so far as in us lies, the wealth of the whole tradition; we learn *from* the Church and we act *as* the Church. We are neither self-righteous critics nor independent self-contained monads — we are participants in the sociality that is the life of the Body.

There is a danger, of course, that this side of Christianity may be stressed in such a way that *all* personal elements are excluded. We have already said that this would be wrong and unchristian. Each of us does have his own part and his own place. But there is a kind of Christian wholeness or totality that is worlds apart from the secularized totalitarianism that destroys the person and denies his particular significance. Totalitarianism asks us to be ants in an anthill; the Christian wholeness or totality does nothing of the sort. *It* asserts that each of us counts; we are not lost or submerged or destroyed in the Church's sociality. Instead, we are given enrichment for our own life; we bring our contribution to the life of the community and from the community we receive a new and enhanced Christian discipleship in common with our brethren. Each member has his own "vocation and ministry"; each branch has its own reality and must bear its own fruit — yet every member, every branch, is organically one with the Body of Christ, the true Vine, so that its hidden contribution and its fruitage are of and for the whole.

In the primitive and early Church, these truths were realized freshly and clearly. To read the accounts of Christian worship, such as those in St. Paul's words in

[65]

I Corinthians, or Justin Martyr's in his *Apology,* or the beautiful description in the *Didache,* or the rite found in Hippolytus' *Apostolic Tradition,* is to be admitted to a scene where the atmosphere of a common faith, a common worship, and a common life, centered upon a common action and bringing to those who took part a sense of common existence, is absolutely pervasive. Here the "feel" of the Body of Christ in all its sociality was both realized and expressed with a vigor and attraction that startle our stilted and sophisticated modern minds.

Individualistic piety, the abandonment of social or collective prayer in the interests of purely "personal" religion, the growth of the secular spirit of individualism outside the Church with its reflection in the realm of the Church's own interior life, worship in a language "not understanded of the people" either in actual words or in idea — these have been suggested as the reasons, historically, for the neglect or perversion of the Christian truth that we are indeed "members one of another" in the Body of Christ. Whatever the historical reasons may have been, it is certainly true that our actual Church practice has often enough done little to make the fact of "membership" clear. Even today there are many Protestant congregations where the plain intention of the great Reformers to have the Eucharist as the chief service for the Lord's people on the Lord's Day has been entirely disregarded or forgotten. In other places the celebrations of the Eucharist have been held according to a schedule rather like that of railway departures: "every hour on the hour," thus destroying any sense of parish solidarity

[66]

and fellowship. These are ways in which we can still suggest an individualistic view of the Christian faith.

But whatever the reasons and however great our failure, the way back to the primitive and early social conception is clear enough. It is by a renewed and continued and insistent emphasis on the Divine Action in human action as the Church's expressive and characteristic work. This is not a matter of what used to be called "churchmanship." On the contrary, it is a matter of Christian integrity and Christian unity. Here is the one place where sociality is so obvious that it is inescapable. Here in the "continual remembrance of the sacrifice of the death of Christ," with all that went before that death and all that followed after it, with the receiving of the holy food that is for "the strengthening and refreshing" of their souls, men can find themselves at one in the unity that is the Body of the Lord Jesus Christ. Happily, the Communion is more and more regarded as at least ideally the main service on Sundays in parishes of all types and denominations.

In the light of the fundamental truth that in this chapter has been argued and urged, we can see why clergy and laymen should work together for the day when each and every congregation will center its life in such worship — in the confidence that from that social action will flow social activity as well as personal dedication. The entire congregation should be together at the Lord's Table week by week; and if this is impossible, very likely the solution is to have smaller parishes or at least parishes that can manage to find ways where such social participation in worship is possible for large groups of the membership. When Christian men and women,

[67]

and children too, gather to recall the offering of Christ for their wholeness or salvation, to offer in union with that gift the entire life of the parish as a token of the entire life of the entire world, to receive back from God in communion the gift of Christ's divine-human life, they will become health-giving, life-giving instruments for God's love in the world. Each parish in this way will come to realize its calling to be a cell in the divine-human organism that is the Body of Christ. Each member of the parish will come to realize his own calling to be an instrument for the redemptive work to which Christ summons us who are his members.

It ought to be apparent that this is no plea for a rejection of Christian activity in the world, in favor of a retreat into the church building for worship and prayer. On the contrary, as the next chapter will show, this is *the way to* significant Christian activity in the world of daily affairs. Many years ago, an acquaintance of the writer was speaking about the way in which so many aspects of modern life had lost their cutting edge. "When you take from anything that which makes it something, what you are bound to have left will amount to nothing" — so my acquaintance phrased it. What he said applies to the Christian enterprise. If we take from it the particular action that gives to Christianity its distinctive quality, we shall have nothing important to contribute to the world. That would be our tragedy. Let us grant that many outside the Church are doing work that makes us ashamed of our own failures. But to admit that is not to say that we do not have something to give. What we have to give is the special quality of loving concern that redeems social activity from mere business and from the condescending goodness that nowadays that wonderful old word "charity" has come to suggest.

For each Christian, realizing his membership in the Body of Christ, the liturgy offers a tremendous opportunity to discover and to implement his Christian calling. Above all, in the Eucharist itself, that opportunity is given. We are not individualistic Christians; we are persons who are knit together in what the Old Testament verse styles "one bundle of life," what St. Paul calls "life in Christ," and what in this book we have named "the en-Christed life." As we take our part in the Church's liturgical action, supremely in the Eucharist, we are formed by the worship in which we engage. What is more, we are enabled to see how we are indeed "members one of another," brethren in the common life that is "in Christ." For the "bundle of life" in which we are knit together is nothing other than the life Christ provides to his people. If it were *only* a matter of our own human existence, we must surely admit, life together might be good and fine, but it would never knit anything together in a permanent fashion, since it is so feeble and broken, so subject to the "changes and chances" that our mortal existence inescapably brings to bear upon it.

But *Christ's* life is another matter. His life, shared with his people, is as strong as Christ himself; it is God's life communicated to men. Its strength is its love — and despite all contrary appearances, there is nothing in the whole world that is stronger than love in action, *a fortiori* God's love in action. Life that is lived "in Christ" has a strength that nothing in our experience can damage; it endures when everything else fails. And

[69]

it is that life, in which Christ dwells in us and we dwell in him, which binds us together, knits us into one, unites us and makes us one in him, even as he is one with the Father. It does more: it takes us, as we are and for what we are, with our imperfection and blindness, our stupidity and our distortion; it redeems us, purifies us, sanctifies us; and then it enables us to live in its own strength, bravely witnessing to Christ in thought and word and deed. The liturgy of the Church exists for just these purposes; and no man can think of himself as an "adequate" Christian unless he humbly, gladly, penitently, but expectantly takes his place in the worship of the Christian fellowship.

6
The Eucharist and Christian Action

In the life of the Christian man and woman *what he is becoming* — his being on the way to realization of his manhood in Christ — is prior to his *activity,* in the sense of outward expression among men of that which his faith implies. Thus the fact that we are members of the mystical Body of Christ, whose goal is the making actual of the possibilities latent in such membership, precedes the correlative demand that we shall act as Christians in the affairs of the world. There can be no question about that demand — for the Christian its imperative is seen in what Jesus had to say about trees that do not bear fruit and which are then good for nothing "but to be cast into the fire and burned." Yet the reason for Christian work in the world is logically, if not always chronologically, found *before* that work is done. Too many of us forget this; and forgetting it, a good deal of Christian activity is more like what the Germans call *Aktivismus* —a kind of crazy running about, which in English idiom is sometimes described by the saying about "chickens with their heads cut off" that engage in galvanic movements that have no meaning or purpose.

Yet, as we have just insisted, it is equally true that

doing must follow upon our coming to know what we *are* and what we have in us to *become*. Such doing follows both logically and necessarily upon the realization of our vocation as living members of the Body of Christ and branches of the true Vine. If we *are* Christians, then we must act like and as Christians. Or we might put it by saying that membership in Christ's Body is not a matter of *status*, given to us for our own enjoyment; it is a matter of *function*, to the end that we may be instrumental in carrying out the work the Body purposes to do in the world. Few things are so pathetic as a useless branch, an inert member of the body; amputation seems indicated in such cases, for when atrophy sets in, the branch or the member can become an impediment to the vine or the body to which it belongs. It is of no use; hence it might just as well be "cast as rubbish to the void."

The relevance of all this to our present discussion is obvious. The Divine Action through human action, which is the liturgy of the Church and which finds its supreme expression in the celebration of the Eucharist, recapitulating as it does the act of God in Christ Jesus and comprehending as it does the "whole mystery of our redemption," *must* lead to Christian action in the world outside the Church itself. But what do we mean when we say "world"?

"World" is a word that is often used very loosely and without much thought. It sometimes suggests an evil place, inimical to God and his purposes. But again it can suggest a good place and the opportunity for responsible action, as when nowadays we hear Christian leaders speak about the need for a "worldly holiness" or a

[72]

"secular" (that is, "worldly") Christianity. This confusion of meaning is found even in the New Testament. Sometimes the "world" is simply the sphere of God's creative activity, hence good; sometimes it is the "enemy" of God and Christians are urged not to "love the world nor the things of the world." Charles Gore, a noted theologian of an earlier generation, once said that in the writings of St. John the "world" is taken to mean human society and the affairs of men as these are organized and oriented apart from conscious relationship to the known will of God. That is part of the truth; yet there are other places in St. John's writings, as well as elsewhere in the New Testament, where a more generous view is implied.

Perhaps we may say that in principle the world is a good place. It is God's creation, which he found "very good." Yet it is always in danger of becoming purely "secular" in the worst sense of that term — that is the truth in Gore's suggestion. But recognition of this must not lead us to call the world, in itself, "evil"; it may "lie in the evil one," as St. John puts it, but that does not make it intrinsically evil.

However this may be, a Christian ought to see that when the affairs of the world are *not* in some way related to God and his purposes, they tend to be so ordered that easily, perhaps almost inevitably, they get into the control of the forces that make towards evil. If we think of the world as a movement or process towards the actualizing of good, rather than as a "finished product" where creation is done and over, we can see that when the creation is not progressing in accordance with God's will towards greater good in shared love, it will slip back into

[73]

indifference, carelessness, self-interest, and self-satisfaction. That will be obvious enough at the level of conscious human life; in differing ways, at lower levels of creation, the same will be seen in the backwaters, drags, or "diminishments" (as we have noted that Teilhard de Chardin puts it), which hold back the movement towards realizing good. There is always the possibility of created elements receiving the allegiance that belongs to God alone; but there is also the possibility of seeing in those created elements the working of God, secretly, hiddenly, anonymously. The former condition is wrong; the latter is right. Recent events in human history teach us this lesson with startling clarity; to labor the point nowadays, in the light of our experience during this century, would be to "carry coals to Newcastle."

Furthermore, from the Christian point of view, this finite order of things in the midst of which we live is not in itself the "kingdom of God." The "kingdoms of this world" are never to be confused with God's reign of perfect love, about which the New Testament speaks in its "eschatological" fashion. God's kingdom can be possible only when and as God's will is perfectly and totally done; that kingdom *is* the reign of Love in the affairs of creation. But the world of here and now, the present world of space and time, is such that the utter completeness of God's reign of love is difficult to conceive, if not impossible to achieve. In any event, what is required for its "coming" is transformation, transfiguration, and reorientation. When the New Testament talks about "the end of the world" and what then will happen, it is speaking in highly symbolic but equally highly evocative pictures of this transformation, transfiguration, and re-

orientation. Underneath the weird, incredible, and sometimes (let us admit it) repulsive imagery used by some
of the writers, the New Testament tells us that this
world, *as it is,* is *not* God's kingdom. At the same time,
it tells us that by God's loving activity it is intended to
become God's kingdom. But certainly not just now —
hence the Christian lives in expectation of the day when
in very truth what he prays for will be achieved: that
God's will shall be done and his kingdom come, "on
earth as it is in heaven."

In any case, despite a very popular misinterpretation,
the New Testament teaching about God's kingdom does
not represent it as a state of mind among men, in which
kind feelings and good intentions are equated with the
fullness of the reign of God. Neither is it taken to be a
state of affairs among men and nations, such as might be
established by human effort on the earth. Both of these
may be desirable, but they are *not* what the Bible means
by God's kingdom. That kingdom is God's own sovereign
rule, although it is a rule in love and a rule by love,
never in coercion or by the exercise of force. Here and
now, in the inner lives of men and in the affairs of the
world, God's love is known and expressed; when that
happens, we have an "earnest," a preview as we might
put it, of his kingdom — in installments, by suggestions,
by intimations.

The task of the Church is not "to bring in the kingdom," as used to be said by older advocates of the "social
gospel"; it is "to prepare and make ready the way,"
which is a different matter. Only *God* can "bring in" or
give us his kingdom; *men* are invited to work with
might and main to conform the affairs of this world,

[75]

and their own lives as well, to the righteous and gracious will of God. They will do this so far as they are able, to the degree that this or that particular situation will permit, in the confidence that in so doing they are indeed preparing, making ready, the way for God himself to act in the world. They are providing the material God can and will use for this purpose. Teilhard de Chardin has written admirably on this subject, showing how such an interpretation of human responsibility for the ongoing of the creative process guarantees both God's sovereignty and the humility with which every human effort must be accompanied if it is not to be presumptuous and ultimately self-defeating.

In the Eastern Orthodox liturgy this is stated with beautiful clarity; and Eastern Orthodox theologians have sought to put the point by speaking of the Church as the likeness of the mother of Christ, while the redeemed creation will also be in her likeness. To unimaginative Westerners this may seem either an absurd or a superstitious idea; or they may reject it as meaningless speculation. But perhaps the Eastern Orthodox are on the right track in this aspect of their theology. For as the mother of Christ was the "chosen" instrument for God's redemptive action in her Son, thus being what traditional theology has called the "consenting cause" of the Incarnation, so the Church may be seen as an instrument whereby God's redemptive activity is also being carried on for men. It is the *ancilla Domini*, "the handmaid of the Lord," in the action of God in the world. And that world, too, as it is redeemed and restored, becomes God's instrument through which he may carry out his purposes of love. Therefore it is also a "handmaid of the Lord"

[76]

for the doing of his will. And it is worth our noting that in each of these — in Mary herself as the New Testament portrays her, in the Body of Christ which is the Church, and in the world as it is to be restored and redeemed — the human work is exactly that "preparing and making ready," of which we have spoken, so that God's will *may* be done.

We have said that it is wrong to think of the world as evil, because it is God's world, created by him, and therefore *must* be good as God is good. Further, it is already in principle redeemed by God in Christ; hence it is truly "very good," even if it is not perfect, even if in its concrete and actual existence it is marked by frustrations, deviations, distortions, and nonconformity with the divine purpose. The world is destined for final restoration, through the power and by the act of God who works in it. This should tell us that the task of the Christian is not, as some have thought, to make the best of what is really a pretty bad job. Such pessimistic thinking will cut the nerve of human effort. Rather, the task of the Christian is "the restoring of all things in Christ," in the noble words of a recent pope. And that is a very different approach from the desperation that marks so much Christian thinking in our day.

In everything that he does, the Christian is the "en-Christed" man who puts his trust and hope in God and in God's unfailing working in the world. He knows that he is called to be a "fellow worker" with God—Whitehead once dared to say a "co-creator" with God, and he was right in saying this — and this cooperation is neither Pelagianism, which would put all responsibility on man, nor extreme Augustinianism, which would put all responsibility on

[77]

God. It is the recognition, in faith, that God works in us and through us, not against us and in spite of us. Hence the Christian does not put his final trust in the world as it is, neither does he expect that with a little tinkering here and a little improvement there it will become perfect. That would be the fallacy of utopianism, a mistake that the events of our time should have shown up for the lie that it is. Precisely because the Christian's hope and trust are in God, not in the world as he finds it, the Christian will not be utterly despairing when failure occurs. He is saved from that despair because *all* of his treasure is not in one basket; he has a "treasure in heaven" — that is, in God himself. The goal he is seeking is not an entirely perfect world, in the natural and limited finite order of things. His goal is in God and in God's perfect will. Yet it is also in *this* world, since God's purpose is to work for just as much expression of the divine love as this world can contain. The Christian will be delivered from wasted effort and from needless anxiety, since he knows from the start that the perfection of God is not attainable short of the eternal kingdom God alone can give.

Yet even if the kingdom of God cannot be entirely contained in the here and now, the created world can increasingly and indefinitely approach towards that end. It can more and more approximate, in more and more places, at more and more times, in more and more ways, and for more and more people, the reign of love and righteousness that is before it as God's plan for his creation. Those who are "in Christ" are called to lend their effort to that movement. We are indeed "fellow workers with God." Nor does this smack of humanism

[78]

in the secularistic sense; let us remember that there is a good and sound and Christian humanism as well as a bad and perverse and unchristian variety. As "fellow workers with God," we are at the same time to remember that "it is God that worketh in us, both to will and to do of his good pleasure." A healthy sense of our own weakness and need is not incompatible with an equally healthy recognition of our divinely given opportunity. The grace of God, given to us through our membership in Christ, becomes our work in the world as Christian men who live "en-Christed" lives.

Sometimes we hear talk about worship as a dynamic towards Christian living, the imperative and the empowering that sends us out to build a new social order. There is truth here, for certainly the new social order must be built, as surely as Christian living is required of us. It is also true that the relationship of worship and work is such that we *are* strengthened by worship for the doing of work. But it is a mistake, a fatal mistake, to think of worship as if it were merely a means towards an end. On the contrary, the worship of God is an end in itself. Not that God "needs" our worship, as if without it he would be impoverished; but rather that it is "good for us to be here," as the disciples said in the presence of the transfigured Lord whom they saw on the Mount "with his garments white and glistening." God must rejoice in our adoration, because he knows that it is good for us to lose ourselves in something that takes us out of ourselves and gives us the joy of living for another. In that sense, we can say that man was created to worship, if by this we mean that he was created to "glorify God and enjoy him forever." Just to be *with*

[79]

one who is loved will satisfy us, as any lover knows. To be with God is satisfaction. But of course it cannot stop there: the adoration must lead to action, although in and of itself the adoration does not exist only as an imperative to that action.

Once this ordering has been noted, we can go on to say that it is also true that our worship provides us with the strength to live Christianly in the world of everyday life and to labor "without rest yet without haste" (as an old prayer says) for the bettering of the place where our lot is cast.

The primary significance of the worship of the Church, and supremely of its eucharistic worship, is that it is a vivid and visible expression, in terms of this world, of the way things are to be in God's intention. When the world is really itself, as God means it to be, it is a liturgy — a public manifestation of God. As the Christian man himself is to be liturgical, an outward and visible expression of God to and in the world, so also that world is to become liturgical, an outward and visible expression of the divine charity.

In worship the right relationship between God and his creation is manifested. The Eucharist shows us the utter dependence of all things on God, the adoration of God through the created order (as in the *Sanctus*), where through men's lips and by their lives they are ready to kneel in his presence, to sing his praise, and to offer to him their oblation of love and service. The created order is here doing what it is meant to do; for heaven and earth are united, living and departed are at one, and the creation is ordered for its own great good and for God's great glory. Man is in his place,

[80]

nourished by the life that comes from God; he is man as God means him to be, the crown of the creation and the image and likeness of God himself. All that he does is related to God as he meets men in Christ and unites them with himself. Sin and failure are forgiven, strength is imparted, a redeemed and transfigured cosmos is both signified and present. Whenever the Body of Christ gathers its members for eucharistic worship, all this is seen, as men worship God the Father through Christ the Son in the power of the Holy Spirit.

The world is meant to be *like that.* Dr. John Robinson has put the matter with splendid clarity in his book *On Being the Church in the World,* especially in the section that talks about materiality, the stuff of things, in relationship to the eucharistic action. And the eucharistic action, properly understood, will lead inevitably to Christian action in the other sense: to work in the world. For Christian action, in *that* sense, is the inspired effort to conform the creation, so far as is possible for it and for us, to the pattern that in the Eucharist is placarded before us.

Thus worship has its anthropocentric consequences, if that is the right way to put it, but essentially it is the great theocentric, God-centered, action of men. It is not man-centered; it is God-centered — and the "man-centered" part is its result. Somebody once asked a member of the Society of Friends who was sitting beside him during the utter silence of a "Quaker meeting": "When does the service start?" The reply came: "When the worship ends." That makes an important point; but in another sense, the worship never ends, since service of God in the world's affairs is also worship. But yet the

[81]

point of worship is not simply to make us better people; that is a by-product, as we might put it. The worship of God is primarily concerned with giving God the glory — and to give God the glory *is* to make us what we are intended to be: his sons, his beloved children. When that understanding is seen as central, when it is at the heart of life and of things, then it will follow, as the night the day, that the Christian will want to bring everything else into conformity with that ennobling vision.

The liturgy helps us to see that we do not need to "go out of this world" to know God; right here in this world, he comes to us. As St. Augustine once said, we are not obliged to climb up into heaven to find the way to God. The way has been brought to us where we are; what we have now to do is walk in it. In this world, where Christ's sacrifice is recalled and his presence received into our innermost being, we have seen heaven. The right and true order of things has been disclosed to us, in terms that are our own: the Divine Action, as we have said, is *in the human action.* That is the principle of incarnation at work in the world; that is how God always acts in respect to his creation. The task we are then compelled and empowered to undertake is to make this world worthy of the heavenly coming. We are indeed the handservants of the Lord who are called to prepare and make ready the way for his coming, so that he can give more and more of himself to more and more of his people at more and more times and in more and more places.

There is still another aspect of Christian action that must never be forgotten. It is called by theologians the "eschatological" perspective. As men in Christ we live ever in two dimensions. We are in the city of man; we are of the city of God. We walk as "strangers and pilgrims" in a world that passes away. For nothing in this mortal existence is eternal and abiding. God will keep all that is good in that existence; in his transfiguring of the creation, as he receives it into himself, nothing that has been achieved will ever be lost. But as Christians we know, what in any case an intelligent man should understand, that the secular realm is not big enough for all that God has put into the human heart. God has made us for himself; he has made us "towards himself," as St. Augustine said centuries ago: hence "our hearts are restless until they find their rest" in God himself. That is why there is and must be a *dis*-ease in man, which is a different thing from, although not unconnected with, the disease or sin that is also in man. There is in every man, however hidden it may be, a strange yearning, a movement, a drive that makes him seek, sometimes almost in spite of himself, for a richer, fuller, truer life beyond "the flaming ramparts of this world." When the Irish poet W. B. Yeats spoke of the "pilgrim soul" of his beloved, perhaps he had this truth in mind.

In a novel of a quarter-century ago, James Ramsay Ullmann caught this note. He tells, in *The White Tower*, of the symbol of the great Alpine peak, which speaks to man of the necessary striving towards the attainment of what seems utterly unattainable and the urge to reach heights far above those to which he has already managed to ascend. Why is this? asks Ullmann. And he answers, "Simply because it is *there*" — that unattained reality, that peak not yet climbed. For Christians, that means God himself, in all his majesty but

[83]

with all his love — and in Christian faith the two are identical, for God's majesty *is* nothing other than his inexhaustible love. So it is, in each man's heart, that

> *Ever and anon a trumpet sounds*
> *From the hid battlements of eternity.*

It is the trumpet of God, calling us to himself.

We could never be satisfied with the most perfect earthly utopia. This is what so many people seem to forget nowadays; but they have against them all the poets, the dreamers, the music-makers, the artists, and the lovers who have ever lived. For the full satisfaction of the human heart, there is required a kingdom "not of this world," in which our broken hearts may be healed, our shattered dreams put together again, our lives knit up, our frustrated desires fulfilled, our God-given humanity irradiated with the light that streams from the divine throne.

Now all this is in the Eucharist, too. Notice that we are not speaking of the contemptible effort of some people to extricate themselves from the world; we are not talking of "pie in the sky when you die, bye-and-bye." We have said bluntly that our action as Christians is to spread the righteousness of God so far as this world of relative justice can contain it. The demand is clearly spoken to it; if we evade response, we are sinners. We are called to share with every man, precisely because we are members of Christ, that which we know; and we are to do everything in our power to make available to others, "in richest commonalty," the boundless charity of God, so far as we are able to give and those others to receive. Unless we do this, we are sinners. But in this

[84]

task, our limit is *heaven;* by which we mean that if we are to be worthy citizens of the kingdom of man, we must first and always be worthy citizens of the kingdom of God into which we have been admitted by our Christian existence as participants in the "en-Christed" life. In no escapist sense, we are to live the life of heaven — the life "in Christ" — in the world of space and time, as colonists and wayfarers. That is our high and hard calling.

It raises frightfully difficult problems. It brings terrible tension and strain in daily experience. It makes Christian action no easy matter. It involves awful and painful conflicts of loyalty and claims to allegiance. There can be and must be tentative and temporary adjustments, resolutions of tension, answers to problems. None of them will be entirely satisfactory as we try to apportion loyalties and claims. But while this must be the case, there will also be the *final* loyalty and the *final* claim; everything else must be recognized as relative. If human living is to be possible at all, we must "compromise" in every area save the *ultimate* one, where *God* lays his claim upon us. At that point, there is no slightest possibility of compromise: "we must serve God rather than men," as St. Peter said when told that he and his fellow disciples should no longer preach Christ. Short of that ultimate claim, it is the genius of Christianity to say that men should never be too well settled in this world, in the realm of the world's immediacies, with all its claims and tensions. To be *too* well settled would be no longer to be on the move; that is the worst treason. To seek after an absolute in this world is to worship a demon; since in this world there are *no* absolutes. But in human experience there is *one* absolute: it is the love of God in Christ Jesus our Lord, which demands from us all we have and all we are.

If Christianity did settle for a temporal and temporary absolute, it would leave man a dull, satisfied, self-regarding earthworm. By depriving him of his striving, his yearning, his forward movement towards God, it would deprive man of his humanity. By letting him find complete contentment in an earthly utopia, it would cheat him of the heavenly hope—life in and with God forever.

> *A man's reach must exceed his grasp,*
> *Or what's a heaven for?*

asked Robert Browning. In saying that, he stated the essential element in what some have mistakenly called "Christian otherworldliness."

Mistakenly, since it is not "otherworldliness" at all. It is simple realism about *this* world, what it is, what it offers, what it can contain. The answer to the yearning of man is the promise of faith: that whatever we have done that is right and good will be received by God, and that we ourselves will be "remembered" by God "for good," as the Old Testament phrase has it. To be taken into God and thus "remembered" by him is the realest of all realities; it is to be absolutely and utterly secure forever, in the only one who *is* "forever," namely, the divine Lover of the world and of men.

As we worship God in the Divine Action of the liturgy, we stand for the moment "in heaven." That is our God-intended destiny. As we are fed with the life of God in Christ, we "eat the bread which came down from heaven." That is our God-given strengthening. The liturgy then leads us out into the world, where we must

[86]

act as Christians, precisely because it does not let us rest content with that world *as it is,* but drives us to acknowledge that we are here as "resident aliens," with a tremendous task imposed upon us. We are to make over that colony in which we dwell until it becomes in truth a "colony of heaven," even while our hearts can never forget and must often yearn for the homeland: *O quanta qualia sunt illa sabbata,* how many and how wonderful are the "Sabbaths" in the life of God into which we are received and where we are eternally remembered "for good."

In one of his bits of obscure Jewish scribal theorizing, St. Paul says all this. He contrasts, in Galatians (4:25-26), the "Jerusalem which now is, and is in bondage with her children" and the "Jerusalem which is above," which is "free and the mother of us all." Because he knew this contrast and lived in terms of its tensions, he could write in another place, "Let the peace of God rule in your hearts, to which also ye are called in one body: and be ye thankful" (Col. 3:15).

7
Life in Christ in the Body of Christ

In this book we have been considering some of the deepest truths about Christian faith and existence. In a way it is all summed up in the well-known Pauline text: "for me to live is Christ." It is the tragedy of the Church's history that the secret of Christian discipleship, expressed in these words, has been forgotten for long periods of time. Then everything has gone dead, Christian faith has lost its attractiveness, Christian worship has become dull and boring, Christian life has become tedious and pedestrian.

Sometimes the business of being a Christian has been represented as accepting a system of beliefs piled one upon another. Sometimes it has been regarded as routine observance of moralistic requirements. Sometimes it has been taken to be a round of meetings for worship, in which nothing very meaningful is said or done. Sometimes, and these have been the worst times, it has been presented to the world as providing a polite veneer for an otherwise decent existence. *Life,* which is the Christian reality, has been forgotten.

Life . . . not life in a biological sense, but "life eternal," life "in Christ," life shared in the mystical Body of

Christ, which is the Church. "He that hath the Son hath life; he that hath not the Son of God, hath not life," so St. John tells us plainly (I John 5:12). The early Christians were often arrested by the Roman authorities for supposedly treasonable beliefs and practices; they were forced to work in the salt mines. There in the mines, suspected of sedition or worse, working under miserable conditions and with insufficient food, they yet knew "life." For on the walls of some of the mines where they performed forced labor, archaeologists today have discovered, written in broken letters, the simple Latin word, *Vita*. "Life" — life in Christ is the secret: it *is* Christianity. To be a member of Christ, to be a branch of the true Vine, to be a partaker of the divine energy that animates the Body of Christ: this is the heart and center of Christianity as a living reality. The theology of the Church is significant only as the basis of that life; the worship of the Church is the expression of that life and the experience of it; the action of a Christian in the world is the externalizing of his inner realization of life. Thus Christianity is "the en-Christed life in the Body of Christ."

In consequence, Christianity is life in charity, life in love, life in fellowship with the brethren. It spreads outwards, diffusing itself like light or like heat, brightening and warming wherever it goes. In any one of us it is not perfect, for we remain creatures prone to sin and liable to failure; nonetheless, it is *towards* perfection because it is towards the perfect Life, which is Christ's life — God's life in man. It is eucharistic life, in thanksgiving to God and in self-offering to him. It is a forgiven life, for there is enough health here to overcome failure

[89]

and sin. The man "in Christ" knows that he is a sinner, but he knows also that the grace of God in Christ's mystical Body is sufficient for him and that his privilege is to live in that grace.

The center of it all, from which his human action springs, to which his human action returns, is his participation, week by week, month by month, year by year, in that *specific* human action in which the Divine Action is disclosed: the Christian "offering of praise and thanksgiving," the Eucharist, where his oblation of himself to God in union with Christ—or more truly, Christ's taking of his members into the context of his "one oblation of himself once offered" — is returned to him in holy communion, where he is fed with the bread and wine of "eternal *life*," so that he may truly be "in Christ."

Let us sum it up in words chosen more or less at random from passages in the New Testament:

"I am the Vine, ye are the branches; he that abideth in me, and I in him, the same bringeth forth much fruit; for without me ye can do nothing" (John 15:5). "That they all may be one; as thou, Father, art in me, and I in thee, that they may also be one in us, that the world may believe that thou hast sent me" (John 17:21). "For we being many are one bread, one body: for we are all partakers of that one bread" (I Cor. 10:17). "For as the body is one, and hath many members, and all the members of that one body, being many, are one body: so also is Christ. For by one Spirit are we all baptized into one body, whether we be Jews or Gentiles, whether we be bond or free; and have been all made to drink into one Spirit. For the body is not one member, but many. . . . Now ye are the body of Christ, and members in particular" (I Cor. 12:12-17). ". . . grow up into him in all things, which is the head, even Christ: from whom the whole body fitly joined together and compacted by that which every joint supplieth, according to the effectual working in the measure of every part, maketh increase of the body unto the edifying of itself in love" (Eph. 4:15-16). "If any man be in Christ, he is a new creature: old things have passed away; behold, all things are become new. And all things are of God, who hath reconciled us to himself by Jesus Christ, and hath given unto us the ministry of reconciliation" (II Cor. 5:17-18).

What has been written in this book is nothing more than a series of meditations on those verses and others like them. In that sense, nothing in these pages is new. Yet in another sense, everything in them is new, since they have been concerned with him who, as an ancient Christian writer phrased it, "is the only new thing under the sun," Jesus Christ our Lord. In his grace and by the working in us of his love, we too can become "new" men and women, by whose reflection of that grace and love the world may be refreshed and a new beauty and glory revealed to the jaded and weary folk of our time.

A Theological Appendix

The Eucharist — Lord's Supper, Holy Communion, "Mass," call it what you will — is or ought to be central in the life of every faithful Christian. For this act of worship both epitomizes and illuminates all that the Christian life is and means. And eucharistic participation, engaged in devoutly, regularly, and dutifully, is much more important than a consideration of theoretical problems that are concerned with how the sacrament imparts to us "the spiritual food of the body and blood of Christ," how that sacrament is in some fashion sacrificial in nature, and the other issues theologians discuss. That we *are* fed with the life of Christ, that he *is* most surely present in the sacrament, and that in truth we *are* identified with his "sacrifice of himself once offered": all these are part of the experience of the devout communicant. The matter of *how* is something else.

But let us not think that it is unimportant. A faith that has no firm rational grounding, an experience that is not susceptible of responsible examination, a life that cannot stand up to inquiry about its nature and validity, are all too likely to become unbalanced or to fade away into mere emotionalism and fantasy. Even if we insist as we must on the secondary role of theological understanding, we can never do without it.

In this appendix we shall consider the theology of the Eucharist, although in so brief a study we can hope only to make suggestions that demand and deserve much fuller and more adequate development. Yet even a brief discussion may have its value. In particular, the approach that will be taken here may be novel to many; and I must begin by saying something about this. My own way of getting at the theology of the Eucharist, as of every aspect of Christian theological understanding, is through the use of "process thought," about which not much was written, and very little was known, in many religious circles until quite recently.

Whatever we say about this matter of eucharistic theology, and of other theological concerns, must necessarily be said in the context of a view of the world, and of God's relation to the world, which to us seems most adequate to the facts of human experience and what we know about that world. No theologian can do his work in a vacuum; he inevitably makes assumptions and has presuppositions — and it is well for him to acknowledge these and make them explicit. Otherwise he is fooling others, even fooling himself. Hence I now write a very few paragraphs whose purpose is simply to inform the reader about my own wider philosophical conceptuality, in terms of which my theologizing is done.

If anything has become evident to thinking people during the past half-century, it is that we live in a world which is evolutionary or "processive" in nature — and I did *not* say "progressive," it should be noted, although many mistakenly assume that evolution and "progress" must go together and therefore charge "process" thinking with an altogether too optimistic outlook, which some slight acquaintance with its exponents would soon show to be a quite erroneous notion of this conceptuality. Most of us nowadays take such a "processive" view for granted. Perhaps it is not quite so evident that we live also in a "societal" world, in which all its elements are interrelated so that everything is affected by and in turn affects everything else. Finally, we are not likely today to think naturally in terms of "substances," or discrete and located *things;* rather, we recognize that the world is composed of events or occurrences. In consequence, the basic question is never what "something" *is,* as it appears to us in some supposedly or apparently fixed form, but *how it goes* — its development or process or movement towards a goal or end.

In such a world, portrayed for us by modern science and intimately experienced by us in our own existence, there are certainly persisting identities; but these are constituted by specific ways in which relationships are brought to focus. Indeed, an event is essentially just such a focus of relationships. We know this to be true in our own lives. John is distinct from his wife and children, his friends, his neighbors, and all that makes up his environment; yet he is not separated from these. He is organic to the so-called "natural creation" and he exists in relationship with others of the human family. To exist as a man *is* to be in such relationship. And what is true of mankind is true more generally in the cosmos; every event in the evolving world is discovered for what it is, as we say, through how it acts in the process of evolving, societal, dynamic reality, even when this is not immediately obvious to us.

One of the main emphases in contemporary theology,

whether explicitly "process theology" or not, is an insistence that for God too this fact of process and relationship and dynamism holds true. There was a time when people could think of God as a "separable" being, isolated from the world and involved in it only as and when it pleased him to intrude into it. The concept of "transcendence" was interpreted in this fashion, although (as we shall see) "transcendence" need not be understood in this way at all. Such a picture of the divine reality makes very little sense to many of our contemporaries. Some of them have taken this to mean that "God has died." But the truth behind that silly assertion is that the picture of a remote, separated God, entirely outside and beyond the world, has "gone dead" for them; and not for them only, but for vast numbers of men and women today. *Another* picture or concept need not fall victim to this mortality.

The interesting point is that a picture of God as distinct from, yet ceaselessly involved in, the world, a picture that stresses movement, relationship, and identity as faithfulness of purpose through changing adaptations to circumstance, is much more biblical than the older picture. A "model" of God as present in the world, really affected by it, and enormously concerned for all its changes and chances, yet consistently himself in the integrity of his character and will, is central in Scripture. This is obviously the case in the Old Testament; and in the New Testament God is declared to be Love, or Lover, who by the necessity of his own loving nature is continually in relationship with the world he both creates and sustains, both loves and guides. Love *is* relationship, as every man knows in his deepest moments of experience; and God as Love and Lover is no exception to this truth. In the scriptural picture we see this God as utterly faithful, utterly unsurpassed by anything not himself, and utterly unexhausted and inexhaustible in his goodness and in his capacity to act in the world out of his own fullness — here is a way of interpreting "transcendence" that makes it significant and important and not an abstract theoretical notion.

Christians proclaim that in Jesus Christ the disclosure of God as loving agent, or active Love, find its focus or climax. He reveals what God is always "up to" in the world; but he does something more than that. Precisely because in him there is a focal and climactic expression in human terms of the divine activity, there is the release of an energy of love (grace) that can bring wholeness or salvation to men, once they learn of it, are grasped by it, and respond to it. When Christians speak of Incarnation and Atonement, this is what they are talking about.

It is in such a context that we can best understand the Christian Church. It is no static institution, no machine for grinding out religious beliefs, no device to produce "religious" people; it is a living fellowship, a "social process," the body of Christ through which its Lord works in a distinctive way to bring his unfailing and gracious presence and aid to his human children. Its identity as Christian is established in its remembering the historic Lord from whom it took its origin, in its continuing relationship to him and to the world it daily seeks to conform to his will, and in its future aim or goal, the kingdom of God for whose coming it is called "to prepare and make ready the way." The Church's

[97]

gospel, its teaching office, its moral principles, its ministry, and its worship are all of them related to and elements in that identity which establishes it as Christ's "mystical Body," whereby the love of God in Christ is actively, vitally, and unceasingly at work.

Of all this the Eucharist is a vivid expression. It too can rightly be understood in the context just outlined; and in that context it *fits*. It fits because in the Lord's Supper the faithful discover the memory of the past originating event in Palestine, their present existence in communion with Christ and in service of the brethren, and their future destiny in the kingdom of God. This pattern of past, present, and future provides for us our first clue to the theology of the Eucharist.

In some form of words or another, the historical liturgies speak of the "continual remembrance" of Jesus Christ — incarnate, crucified, risen — effected in the eucharistic action. The reference is to the past but not as if it were a *dead* past. "Remembrance" is not the simple retrospective look; it has to do with the bringing of the originating events into the immediacy of contemporary experience. Like the memory of the Passover in the Jewish *seder,* the eucharistic remembrance is no matter of archaeology but is the way in which contemporary believers are grasped by that which has happened to bring them into existence as a community of faith and set them upon the path of loyal discipleship.

In the present moment, communion with the risen Lord is made available to the communicant as "with faith and thanksgiving" he receives the elements that, according to the Lord's command, have been "taken in memory" of him. The whole Christ — Jesus as a historical figure and Jesus as the living Lord, raised from the dead and known as still mediating the divine love to men — is present for the faithful. His "presentness" to their faith, in eucharistic communion, is the meaning of what we call his "presence" in that action; and having thus been made present, the same Lord sends his disciples out into the world, with the mission of bringing into every area of that world's experience the life that is nothing other than love-in-action.

As to the future stress, we can see once again that the historical liturgies unfailingly speak of the coming of the kingdom of God, in which both divine purpose and human aspiration will be fulfilled and completed. But as the past is not a dead past, so this future "coming" is not entirely remote and (so to say) merely at the end of time. The "powers of the age to come" are already present; the "first fruits of the Spirit" are already known. The worshipper is enabled to share now in what might be styled an anticipatory or preliminary participation in the kingdom that is not yet fully and completely here. Before "the time," he enjoys this sharing in "the time"; and he enjoys it in this present world where his life is being lived out.

Thus the identity of the Eucharist is established by memory, relationship, and future aim. The "continual remembrance" of the *past,* the *present* communion in the Lord's "presentness" with the mission to be carried out, and the *future* coming of the kingdom already enjoyed in anticipation: here is eucharistic identity. And what it comes down to is exactly what St. Thomas Aquinas, in a quite different connection, said about the sacrament: it is both the "summary of the mystery of

[99]

our salvation" and the reality of the *totus Christus,* "the whole Christ." In Christ's "presentness" we are given no *thing* but a vital relationship of Lord and people, uniting God's action in the past, his promise for the future, and the urgent and empowering strengthening in the present. The human celebration at the hands of men is caught up into and made effective through the divine action of God's self-giving in his Son.

Since it is the *whole* Christ who makes himself present, the "presentness" is necessarily Christ *in his wholeness.* That is to say, here is the inclusive Christ, with all that he was and is, did and does, meant and means. The sacrificial offering of himself throughout his earthly life was brought to its climax in his sacrifice of himself on Calvary, to do the Father's will as he understood it, and to do this on behalf of those whom he called his brethren, so that they might have the life "which is life indeed." So, in his "presentness" there is present the reality of the sacrifice he made. This is why it is entirely appropriate to speak with Catholic Christianity and with the Wesleys of the Eucharist as marked by a sacrificial character — yet we can thus speak only provided we do not presumptuously think that it is *we* who offer Christ, but remember that it is *he* who offered himself to the Father and with himself offered all who are "very members incorporate" in him and indeed, by the extension of his love, all men anywhere and everywhere who are bound together with him in the nature and lot proper to human existence.

In past ages discussions of the theology of the Eucharist have been bedeviled by a philosophy that thought in terms of located "substances" or "things." We have seen

[100]

that this view is not really biblical and we now know that it is not in accordance with the facts of the case. The world is constituted of events in process, with rich social relationships that make them what they are. That newer view delivers us once for all from a "thing" conception of reality and hence from the need to think of the Eucharist in a "thing" way.

We can readily see why the medievals, in their desire to stress the reality of the Lord's presence in the eucharistic action, were led to speak of the replacement of one "substance" by another, in the Lord's Supper. If Christ were indeed present through bread eaten and wine drunk, somehow his "substance" must be made to take the place of the "substance" of the natural elements, even if the outward appearances (the "accidents") were not altered. This was the doctrine of transubstantiation, of course. In reaction to it, Lutheran scholastic theology (but not Luther himself), still victim to a "substantialist" outlook, held that the new "substances" of Christ's body and blood were present alongside or "with" (and "through" and "under") the bread and wine. This was consubstantiation. John Calvin in some respects did better, for although he still spoke of "substance," he saw that it was better to say that through the Spirit's gracious activity the believing communicant was taken up into heaven, there to feed on the heavenly body and blood of Christ. The extreme Reformers would have none of these theologies; some of them, perhaps including Zwingli, had almost but not quite a purely "mental" presence, thereby coming near to denying any "presentness" of Christ *in the action itself.*

It is the contention of this appendix that with the col-

[101]

lapse of the older view that talked of "substances" in a definite location, and the coming of a newer view that works with ideas such as event, occurrence, process, and societal interrelationship, we no longer need to worry so much about how *this* "thing," in *this* place, at *this* time, can serve as instrumental for spiritual realities. We must speak of a here and now (a time and space, if you will) but we need not speak of a "thing." Every event in the universe is in relation to every other event; spatiality and temporality are media for such "presentness" of whatever is going on, happening, taking place. And God himself is related to a space-time world, involved in it, self-identified with it. The risen Lord who is "with the Father" can be present as an event whose effects are felt and known in that here and now, more particularly as and when faithful response is made to him. This is the deep truth, incidentally, of the Prayer Book's declaration that it is "by faith," by human response in commitment, that we are brought to know the Lord's presence in the Supper.

It is not surprising, perhaps, that some anticipations of this interpretation of the Eucharist, theologically speaking, were advanced in older days. In St. Augustine's remarks about symbols, or "signs of sacred realities," and about the "mystery of yourselves" (the Christian Church's members) upon the altar, one aspect is hinted at. In the Alexandrine Fathers' platonizing view of sacraments something of the same sort appears. Berengar of Tours is interesting in his theory of "dynamic symbolism," as it has been called. And when Aquinas writes that the *res* of the sacrament is "the unity of the Church" he quite unconsciously stresses our insistence on the societal context of the sacrament. John Calvin is notable for his "virtual" or dynamic view of presence by the Holy Spirit. Each of these bears witness, in his own way, to the enduring experience of Christian believers that their Lord somehow is present to them in the sacred meal; so does the long history of Christian worship and the astounding capacity of this rite to awaken and deepen faith in a Lord whose "presentness" is vividly if mysteriously known. For the Lord's Supper has been the abiding nourishment of the life in grace, just as it has also shown itself to be (in Wesley's words) "a converting ordinance."

Any theology of the Eucharist must account for this awareness of "presentness" and for the fact that it is indelibly associated with the bread and wine that are taken and consumed. Of course these elements are symbols, as a platonizing view would hold; but they are also *effectual* symbols that accomplish what they signify. A "substance" philosophy finds it difficult to speak of such effectuality, since it is oriented in a quite different direction. It is just here that the "event" type of thinking comes to our aid. By its use we can relate the effectuality to the elements without succumbing to almost magical ideas of transformation; and when to it we add the emphasis on social relationships we can make some approach to understanding how we have to do with more than "mental" presence, how indeed we have to do with a social "presentness" that provides a context for the specific focus in the use of the bread and wine.

When we speak, as we do, both in liturgical words and in personal prayer, of the bread and wine as being "the spiritual food of Christ's body and blood," or (in better language) the instrumental agency through which

[103]

that food is given and received, what do we mean? We mean that the universal cosmic Love that is personified as God himself — and not by our theorizing but by the very fact of love's personalizing quality — has been brought near to us and dwelt among us in the human loving that was Jesus. We mean that this same Jesus is made present in his very innermost reality, his "very self" if you will, to his faithful people as they "do this in remembrance" of him. We mean that his disciples live in him and he in them. And we mean that by this participation they are empowered as God's children to become the lovers God intends them to become. The whole action is neither magical nor mental, but total, vital, all-inclusive and all-compelling.

But as I said at the beginning, the theological interpretation is not the essential point, important as it is. The one thing about the Eucharist that ultimately matters is our fellowship in and through it with the Lord himself and by him with our brethren also. The simplest person — the "charcoal burner," as Pasteur said — is equal here to the most learned of theologians. Perhaps sometimes he is in a better case than the theologian, since it is to the pure in heart, not to the clever in mind, that God promises to disclose himself.